MW01488710

70-30 Split

A Practical Guide to Blend Motivation, Leadership and Coaching

Gerald Brence

The 70-30 Split

Copyright ©2010 by Gerald Brence

All rights reserved. No part of this book may be reproduced in any form without permission in writing from the author, except in the case of brief quotations embodied in critical articles or reviews.

1st Edition 2009
2nd Edition 2010

ISBN 978-1-61658-738-3

www.geraldbrence.com
books@geraldbrence.com

Hodge Printing Company, Dallas, Texas

Printed in the United States of America

Dedication:

I dedicate this book to my wife, Beth, and my three sons, Ryan, Beau, and Collin. Thanks to everyone I have competed with or against through the years.

The 70-30 Split

Gerald Brence

Gerald Brence

The 70-30 Split

"Build up your weaknesses until they become your strong points."
---Knute Rockne, football coach

The basic makeup for an athletic team depends 70% on the athlete. The other 30% relies on the influence of coaching. As the season moves on and the competition level gets higher, the split tightens. When peak performance is realized, the split may be all the way down to 51% the competitor and 49% the coaching. However, the tilt will never go in favor of the coaching. It will always tilt toward the players. Individual drive is always the most important ingredient, but coaching is the wild card that often makes the difference. The trick is to figure out how to balance the split.

Recognize all the factors. If you are going to take on a new leadership role, you better understand one thing very quickly. You can't control everything. Players play at different levels. The team or organization that has the better players should win. However, they often don't. There are many reasons for success or failure. It is difficult to comprehend. Write down a list of all the factors that will make a difference in your task. Develop it into a chart.

The "Player's Coach" theory is overrated. I never put much stock into a coach being really close to his players. I always wanted coaches, not big brothers. A good coach has a solid relationship with every player. Fairness is the most important factor. Team morale will suffer if a coach gets close to some players but is distant from others. I heard Tom Landry speak at a clinic one time. He talked about the great competition to be the Dallas Cowboys quarterback. I remember him asking us a question. "If I was in the weight room after practice talking to one of the quarterbacks, do you think the other one wasn't watching from across the room?" Coach Landry chose to be more aloof and distant from the players when he became the head coach. He felt it was the only way that made things fair for everyone.

Think hard about the toughest decisions. One of the toughest decisions a coach must make is how hard to work his team. The great ones find that fine line between working the players too hard or not hard enough. They get conditioning just right. You want the players fresh, but they must have their legs at the end of the game. If you don't work them hard enough, they will falter at the end.

Simplicity vs. Complexity. The more people you involve, the more chance of a mental error. Keep things as simple as possible, but you must scheme some. You have to factor in the athletic ability of your players. Usually, simple wins out in the end. There is an old saying in the coaching business, "When you get in trouble, simplify."

Athletic ability vs. scheme. It is a fact that some players are just smarter than others. Many times the coach has to pick between a cerebral player and an athletic one. Again, the athletic player usually wins out, but it isn't a given. The coach has to think it through and decide what he wants.

Evaluate and think long term. After every game the coach and his staff should break down every play that occured in the game. That is how you can really look at your team and decide the direction you need to go. A lot of coaches get caught up in what **they** know. That isn't what is important. What is important is what the **players** know. One of the great things about sports is that we use a scoreboard. You will know how you did after every game. Start looking at the 70-30 split theory, and see how it affects your view of the team.

The 70-30 Split

Table of Contents

CHAPTER 1
Motivation

70% players	30% coaches

General MacArthur's View

"Concentrate, play your game, and don't be afraid to win."
---Amy Alcott, professional golfer

People have different views on the importance of athletics. Many feel that the emphasis on sports is way out of whack. Look at the issue on a deeper level, and make your own judgment.

Realize that the emphasis on athletics can get distorted.
Athletic teams are vehicles to support the academic program of the school. When a tough problem arises about a student/athlete, ask a simple question. "What is in the best interest of the student academically?" The question helps parents, teachers, and coaches out of some delicate situations.

Parents play the key role. We must educate parents to correctly emphasize sports. Integrity is the most important thing. When a student/athlete understands this concept, he or she is set up for success.

Highly competitive games with a lot at stake can be one of the best training tools in education. The opportunity to participate in a huge event with pressure involved is a great opportunity that should not be taken lightly.

Recognize the value of athletics. Kids learn team synergy, work ethic, time management and many other skills in athletics. One of the most important things that athletics teaches people is the least understood. Athletic competition gives people a chance to learn and practice leadership skills.

Look at the big picture. Douglas MacArthur was born in Little Rock, Arkansas. His father was a famous general who joined the Union Army and fought in the Civil War. Of course, Douglas grew up in the Army. His dad was gone most of the time. When Douglas entered the United States Military Academy at West Point, his mother went along with him. The story goes that she checked into the Thayer Hotel on campus, and she didn't check out until Douglas graduated four years later.

The stories of hazing that Douglas went through at West Point were legendary. Upperclassmen were especially hard on the young cadet. However, he never complained.

Douglas was a small guy, but he loved athletics, especially football. He wasn't big enough to play, so he became the team manager. He saw up close and personal the value of being on a sports team.

Douglas graduated in 1903 as the leading man in his class. He then started his military career. In 1919, he became the superintendent at West Point. He began by expanding the academy's curriculum and raising standards in every category. Douglas was heavily involved in athletics. It was his belief that if the academy wanted to recruit the best of the best, they needed to focus on recruiting athletes.

Army upgraded all their athletic programs. The football team became a powerhouse in the 1940's with great players like Doc Blanchard and Glenn Davis. West Point began competing at the highest level in every varsity sport.

It didn't finish there. MacArthur instilled the concept that "every cadet is an athlete." If a cadet did not compete in a varsity sport, he was required to compete in intramurals. MacArthur also believed that the Physical Education department should be as respected as the Math department. He stressed that cadets should be well rounded in physical, academic and military skills. General MacArthur did a lot of great things during his lifetime. One of them was to push the emphasis on athletics in America.

Suit up for the Game

"Enthusiasm, backed by horse sense and persistence,
is the quality that most frequently makes for success."
---Dale Carnegie, motivational speaker

Higher enthusiasm leads to more energy. More energy leads to more fun. More fun leads to more success. It only takes some planning and a little work. Take control of your attitude by taking control of the way you present yourself.

Stay in touch with your rules. Making the best presentation of yourself goes much deeper than how you look. People will be watching you. In a proper work environment there is no place for profanity, name calling or sarcasm. Set specific rules to follow when you are in the workplace, and then don't cross the line. Office gossip is for somebody else, not you. Never speak negatively about a co-worker. Place your standards high, and stick to your plan.

Leave it better than you got it. There is an old saying, "When the boss is away, the mice will play." In many places, maybe that's the way it works. However, that goes against what any strong leader is actually trying to accomplish. When the boss is away things should move along the same as always. Great leaders prepare others to lead. The day you start a leadership position you should start looking for your replacement. Train your people to be better, more organized, more motivated employees. Create an environment where your people want to come to work. When you are away, they can assume leadership positions. When you leave the position, make sure you leave it better off than when you got there.

Don't wait for someone else to set the standard. The famous quarterback of the San Francisco 49er's, Joe Montana, tells a story about a rookie wide receiver. Montana remembered the first day of practice early in his pro career. All the veteran players showed up for practice in shorts. This rookie wide receiver appeared in full pads game apparel. It was obvious the rookie took a lot of time getting his uniform just the way he wanted. His socks were perfect. His sweat bands were clean and fitted. His towel hung just right off his belt. Many of the veteran players smirked at him.

The rookie got to the front of the line. Joe threw him a five yard hitch. The ball hit the rookie in the facemask and bounced away. Three minutes later, the rookie got back to the front of the line. Joe threw him another pass. Again, it bounced off his hands and onto the ground. Montana remembered the pros laughing and saying, "He won't last till the water gets hot."

The rookie got to the front of the line a third time. This time when Montana threw him the ball, he caught it. His eyes followed the ball into the cradle of his outside arm. He tucked it away perfectly. He then looked up and started sprinting downfield. He ran full speed down the sideline and crossed the goal line.

It was obvious that he knew the fundamentals of his position. He finally stopped at the back of the end zone. He knew everyone was watching. The entire team suddenly sensed that he might be something special. The rookie wide receiver's name was Jerry Rice. He became one of the greatest players in NFL history.

Speech of Fire

"Never apologize for showing emotion. When you do so, you apologize for the truth."
---Benjamin Disraeli, British prime minister

It has been my experience that fiery speeches are usually overrated. However, they do have their place. The trick is to learn how to use them.

When inspiration is needed, choose positive information over passionate nonsense. Most games are a marathon not a sprint. The hype and excitement will only last so long, and then substance takes over. When you need a difference-making speech, you better be prepared, and you better be at your absolute best.

Long term motivation beats short term motivation. You can help your team in a much larger way by being totally organized in your motivational approach. I believe in long term motivation. You must set a base to your expectations. Select three base goals you want to accomplish. Talk about them often. Put together groups of smaller goals that support your base goals. Think it all through well before the season starts. Long term goals will have substance and will pull you through tough times.

Rely on passion only when it comes directly from your heart. You will know when to use fiery speeches and what to say if it comes straight from your heart and instincts. Just before kickoff on Friday night I always told our players the same thing. I told them that the most important thing for them was to put God first in their lives.

One big game I got all fired up and made this passionate speech.

I went on and on about how we had to be physical, hold onto the ball and play great defense. I looked at one of our offensive linemen. "All that is important, but what is the most important thing of all?" I asked him. He looked at me calmly and said, "Put God first in your life." I looked at him for a few seconds and then said, "I'm getting to that, but right now I'm talking about the kicking game!"

Coaching the Coaches

"Don't cry because it's over. Smile because it happened."
--Theodor Geisel (Dr. Seuss) author

One subject that can be very touchy is the issue of dressing appropriately for work. You will get all kinds of views on this subject. Before you say something you regret, you better think it through.

Realize the problems that people have with clothes. When I was a very young coach I confronted this big offensive lineman about the way he dressed for school. I brought him in and told him that he should put more thought into what he wore.

Later that night his mother called me. She was thankful that I took the time to counsel her son, but she explained why he dressed the way he did. He was around 6'4" and 250 pounds. She explained to me that she couldn't find clothes to fit him. Besides that, she couldn't afford the high cost of keeping him in clothing, because he was growing so fast. She did the best she could. It was quite a lesson for me.

You need to realize that everyone isn't a fashion mogul. There are physical and financial reasons that dictate the way people dress. There are also cultural reasons, and don't forget that people just have diverse ideas about style.

Work hard to help people. If you are in a leadership position, you can find a way to help people with clothing. Study and shop for shirts, jackets and even pants that you can buy for your entire staff. I know it is expensive, but if you have a problem this is a way to solve it. But beware; your opinion on style won't always match the office staff. At least you can make an effort. They will appreciate it, and it should make a difference. For some employees you can even create a uniform for them to wear to work.

Look for the humor in it all. We always had a great rivalry with Duncanville High School when I was coaching at Plano. Their longtime coach, Bob Alpert, was one of my favorite people. He was hilarious. I don't ever remember having such a fun relationship with an opposing coach.

In the spring time, we all would go to each other's spring football games. One year our entire staff got to Duncanville well before the start of their spring game. Bob was out on the field watching the junior varsity scrimmage. He had broken his leg coaching an all-star game and was sitting in a golf cart at midfield.

I told the coaches, "I'm going to walk out there and talk to Alpert." I walked out to the middle of the field, and he was thrilled to see me. At least he acted like it.

We always needled each other pretty sharply. I looked at all the Duncanville coaches. Their school colors were red and blue. The coaches were dressed in all kinds of different arrangements. Some were in t-shirts, others in old sweatshirts.

We never won any fashion awards while I was the coach at Plano, but I just couldn't resist. "Man, I thought we looked ragged. You need to assign a fashion coordinator for your staff." I was just joking. Bob started lecturing me on how that kind of stuff didn't matter. I laughed it off and forgot about it.

A year passed before Dan Schrieber, Bob's offensive coordinator, told me what happened next. Alpert came in the office the next day and jumped all over the Duncanville coaches. "We have to clean up our act and get some new workout gear. Brence said we look like crap."

I have never met a coach that didn't like to get new gear. Schrieber ordered all new shirts, shorts and even some new Nike shoes for the entire staff.

A few days went by when some of the coaches noticed that the head man wasn't wearing his new shoes. Schrieber asked him about it. Bob went into his office. He came out and pitched a box of shoes on Schrieber's desk. "Send these back. They're too small. They hurt my feet."

Schrieber went back to his desk and examined the shoes. Then he got up and went back into Alpert's office. "Coach," he said. "You have to take the paper out of the toes before you try them on."

The Concrete Thought

"Your intellect may be confused, but your emotions will never lie to you." ---Roger Ebert, critic

In order to get something done you need to envision the end of the project. When you reach a point that you know the project will be finished, it becomes a "concrete thought." You know it will be finished, you just don't know the time table. In athletics, business, or any other endeavor this type of thinking turns you into a high achiever.

Leaders are dreamers. Have the courage to follow through on your idea. Dream it all the way out in your mind. If you can visualize it, you can accomplish it.

Handle skepticism correctly. Don't give up so easily on your dream. Others will tear down your dream with negativity or skepticism. Listen to them, but don't give in to them. Be more determined than ever to make your project succeed.

Realize that it is a spiritual thing. If something is coming through your heart so strong, you need to recognize it as such. There is a reason for you to see it to the end. Trust your instincts. Follow your yearning.

You need to see it. One day I went into an office supply store. I saw an odd stack of books. These books had no wording inside. They were just blank. They were also just the size of the book I envisioned publishing. I bought a couple of them. I went back to my computer and started writing the current format. I would print what I wrote, cut it down to size to fit the book, and then I glued it onto the pages. All of a sudden, it was something I could see and touch. I now knew what my book was going to look like at the end. I knew it was going to be a reality some day. All I had to do was follow through with my plan. It became a "concrete thought."

Motivate the Team and the Individual

"My main job was to develop talent. I was a gardener providing water and nourishment to our people. Of course, I had to pull out some weeds, too."
--Jack Welch, executive

The ability to motivate people is vital to success. Many leaders just don't study motivation enough. Motivation is tied to morale, and morale is the backbone of every organization.

Focus on the relationship you have with the entire team as a whole. What is the mood and the morale of your team? Do your subordinates like and respect you? What do you do that might cause problems in the workplace or on the field. Are you giving them clear direction? If you are the leader, you better think about these things. You don't have to be buddy-buddy to be a strong leader. However, you do have to have the respect of the people in your organization.

Make sure everyone knows your three main objectives. This is a recurring theme in this book. Make sure everyone from the top to the bottom knows the three main things you want to get done. Some leaders don't know one. Post the three goals. Talk about them openly and often. It will bring everyone together.

Create vehicles to help you lead. Brainstorm and figure out a vehicle to help you. Develop a workshop. Create a seminar. Think of a way to bring people together so you can talk to them and promote your agenda. You don't have to make it mandatory. Bring food into the project. That always works.

Focus on the individual. Work hard at individual relationships with everyone. That way you have a relationship with the team and a relationship with the individual. Again, you don't have to be everybody's best friend. Just communicate with people on a human level. A smile, a yes, sir, or a friendly handshake will go a long way with a subordinate. Just because you are the boss doesn't make you a big shot in his eyes.

Be Approachable. It is critical that your people feel they can approach you. Go out of your way to make people feel comfortable around you. Your team needs to know and feel that you care about them. Of course, if you want to be a hard core leader with no warmth it's your business. It just usually doesn't work out in the long run.

Bruce Juice

"The first thing a great person does is make us realize the insignificance of circumstance." --Ralph Waldo Emerson, poet

Some of the best memories in life come from emotional moments. Capitalize on emotion, and you will do great things. You just have to keep things under control. The great stories are stamped on your heart like a tattoo.

Don't be afraid to show emotion. It's important to be cool and calm, but there is also a time to show how you really feel. People need to know that you care. It needs to be real. Raw emotion is powerful.

Corral it into your plan. It is smart to factor emotion into your plan. Remember to save it for when you really need it. Many times you burn yourself out before the big moment arrives. Save your emotion for the start of the game.

Personalize it. Bruce Springsteen, the rock and roll legend, tells a great story. When he was just a young teenager, he told his mother that he saw a guitar down at a local pawn shop. It cost $69. He told his mom that if he could somehow buy that guitar, he could get a job and help her pay some bills.

Time passed by. On his birthday, mom walked into the room and said, "Bruce, let's go buy that guitar." When she got to the counter to pay, she pulled out $69 in cash. It was the most money Bruce had ever seen in one place. The guitar was roughed up a bit, but it was rock solid.

The next time you see Bruce Springsteen, look really close. There is a good chance he is using that same guitar his mother bought for him down at the pawn shop.

The 24 Hour Prayer

"God doesn't care about your ability.
He only cares about your availability."
---Mary Kay Ash, business executive

The basic theme of this book is to trust your instincts and be your own leader. To to that you need to have strong faith. If you ask for guidance, you will get it. You will receive it through your instincts. That is one way that God talks to you.

Make the most important thing the most important thing. You hear this quote from a coach all the time. "I put God first in my life. I put my family second, and I put my job third." A lot of kids really struggle with that statement, because they aren't exactly sure how to put God first in their lives. I decided as a coach to address that statement.

What if the first thing you did when you popped out of bed was to start your day in prayer? It isn't hard. Make it short and to the point. Write it down if it helps. Just make sure you start your day the same way every day. Isn't that putting God first?

It's about consistency not volume. You will be much happier and successful are consistent. Many people get fired up for a couple of weeks about faith, and then they forget about it. Keep it simple, and be consistent.

Start with thanks. No matter who you are, you are a blessed person. Start off your day by giving thanks for all you have. The rest will come easy.

Think about others. It will make you feel better about yourself. Remember, there are people in very tough situations that need your help. You can help them if you pray for them.

Be specific. Tell God what is bothering you and what you want. Just remember that he will answer on his own terms and with his own timing. The line is open all the time, and you will never get a busy signal.

Understand Faith. John Wooden, the great UCLA basketball coach, developed his own pyramid of success. Faith was a major factor. He explained his view on what it meant. He stated, "Faith is the belief that things are going to turn out the way they should."

Sunday is about a lot of things. There are a lot of reasons to go to church. My wife and I had three boys. Sunday morning was always a test for me to see how they dressed, what they looked like, and how they acted. Plano, Texas was a fast town. Sunday morning was always a time to slow down.

Break bread with your loved ones. During spring break one year, we lost two players in a terrible car wreck. At one of the funerals, I was visiting with a grieving mother. She told me the story about her two boys, one of which she had just lost. She would roust them out of bed every Sunday morning. They always went to church together.

After church, they went to eat. Often, mom couldn't afford it, but she took them to a restaurant anyway. She knew if she fed them, they would talk to her. She said that she savored those lunches. She knew her boys knew God. In the absolute worst of times, at least she knew that.

Personalize your Daily Workout

"How old would you be if you didn't know how old you were?"
--Satchel Paige, baseball pitcher

There are two things we all have in common. Time is going to pass, and things are going to change. As we get older, it is important to point out that it is critical to keep moving. Procrastination on exercise and a sedentary lifestyle are the two biggest enemies. An organized workout plan is tough to follow for anyone. It is especially hard on people who burn the candle at both ends. However, there are ways to make it productive and enjoyable. You just need to be organized and motivated.

It's about consistency not volume. A lot of people will get fired up to workout and then flame out after about a week. You must overcome that kind of thinking. Keep things simple. Make sure you don't change your lifestyle much, especially at first. You are much better off to start very slowly. Be consistent with what you choose. Don't load up with some complicated workout. If you do too much, you increase the odds against yourself. Start off with something pretty easy that you know you can do every other day. **Create a workout system that becomes the highlight of your day.** That is how to make it a success.

Write it down. All kinds of studies have shown that if you write down what you will do in your workout you have a much greater chance for success. Be very specific in what you choose to do. Look for the right time and place to execute the workout. Just keep it simple.

Realize that you will get immediate results. People often don't start a workout program, because they think they are just too far gone physically. They think it will take months before they will see results. The opposite is actually true. You will get immediate results the day you start. It is really amazing what a small workout can do for you.

Find your niche. I always do things in threes. For example, find an inexpensive curl bar and some light weights to fit it. Put it in your garage, backyard, or wherever you can get to it easily. Don't worry about dressing out in workout gear. Just pick up the curl bar and do 10 curls. Put it back on the ground and flip your hands around. Pull the bar up to your chin 8 times. That is one set. For the second set do 8 curls and 6 reverse curls. For the third set do 6 curls and 4 reverse curls. That's it. Try to do it every day. Your body will tell you when to take a day off. You will be surprised how quickly you will see results.

Work your core. I wish I would have started working my abdominals when I was a kid. I just didn't care about it that much back then. Now that I'm older, it is the center of all my workouts. There are all kinds of gizmos and machines to work your abs. Find one that doesn't hurt when you use it. Then wear it out.

Keep moving. You don't have to run 5 miles every day to get cardiovascular work. You just need to move. Do something you enjoy. Mow the lawn. Clean the garage. Take a hike. Just find something physical to do. I enjoyed the HBO series John Adams. During the mini-series, John was constantly doing physical labor on the family farm. In one of the last scenes, he was out pitching hay with a pitchfork. He was into his 90's. Now he didn't have a great body, but he was in good condition.

Try sprinting instead of running distance. Pick out a distance of say 50 yards. Run the best you can for the 50 yards. Walk back to your starting point. As you walk back implement a breathing exercise. Inhale through your nose a deep breath. When your lungs are full take three short sniffs. Then exhale until your lungs are empty. Follow through with three short exhale breaths. Breathing exercises are great for you. This is a tremendous exercise routine for anyone. A lot of people just don't like running long distance. Your body is like anything else. Use it or lose it.

The Blue Note Card

"When fortune smiles, embrace her."
--Thomas Fuller, historian

Good things happen to those who wait. This is especially true when choosing your husband or wife. Young people feel all kinds of stress dealing with the dating game. Here are some ideas on how to take the pressure off.

Stop taking things so seriously. There is plenty of time for a young person to get serious about a boyfriend or a girlfriend. Develop the right mindset. View boys and girls equally as your friends. Don't get caught up in the drama of it all.

Look down the road. Throughout high school and college you will meet literally hundreds of new people. Put it in God's hands, and quit worrying so much about romance.

Trust your instincts. I grew up in Cordell, Oklahoma. I always loved the Oklahoma Sooners football team. When I was twelve, an OU football player named Eddie Foster came to speak to our Fellowship of Christian Athletes group. The meeting was at the First Baptist Church. It was the middle of winter on a Saturday night. I came down with the flu. I had a high temperature and was sick in bed all day. However, I was not going to miss meeting an OU football player.

I got up and walked down to the church. Eddie was an offensive tackle. He was a huge guy. His main points were about young people and dating. He told us that our future husbands and wives were out there somewhere, and that we should honor them even though we might not even know them now. He said we should establish a relationship with God and pray about our future mates.

Then he told us that if we would do that, God would bring us our mate when he felt the time was right. In the meantime, Eddie told us not to worry about dating. He told us that we would know instinctively when we met our mates. "You will just be able to tell," he told us.

Obviously, he made a big impression on me. Several years passed by. I moved to Texas to start my coaching career. One day a female teaching friend of mine told me she wanted me to meet her buddy. "No," I said. "I don't like blind dates." She said okay, but she would put her friend's phone number in my mailbox anyway. I checked my mailbox, and sure enough there was a blue note card with a phone number on it. I put the note card in a book and placed the book in my library.

Another year passed. This same friend saw me in the hallway one day. "Hey, did you ever call my friend?" I explained that I was too busy and never called. "Well, you should call her," she said. "I will put her phone number in your mailbox." "Don't bother," I replied. "I still have it."

I decided to get the note out and call her. I could tell the first time I spoke to her on the phone that she was special. I could just tell. A year later, I proposed. I carried that blue note card in my wallet for years. I finally had to have it laminated, because it was falling apart. It all happened just like Eddie Foster said it would.

Coaching the Coaches 2

It's important to take care of everyone in your organization. You better pay close attention to the stars, but you also better pay attention to the role players. Leaders had better be aware of and appreciate everyone around them. You never know who could be the key to your success.

Build your team from the bottom up instead of the top down. Strong leaders care about everyone. All it takes is a little extra effort. Make sure you know everyone's name. Make sure that not only you but everyone else in your organization treats the low level employees with respect.

Go the extra mile to foster relationships. Spend quality time with your lower level employees. Get to know them. Never come off as uppity or arrogant. If you are a coach, you are only as good as your weakest player. You better pay attention to him just like your top player.

Have fun with everyone. David Odell is famous at Plano Senior High School. He played on the state championship football team in 1977. After he graduated the school district put him to work washing uniforms and cleaning up trash around the field house at the senior high school.

David took great pride in being a preacher. He often practiced his sermons while he was working. Many people thought he talked to himself, but I knew he was just practicing his sermons. Of course, a lot of the kids and most of the coaches picked on him, but David had a sharp tongue. Few people ever got the last word in on him. He didn't value being well groomed, and he took a lot of abuse for it.

In late July, David and I were often the only people on campus at Plano Senior High. One day my wife's car was in the shop, and I needed a ride to go get it. I asked David if he would take me to the car dealership.

We walked over to his car, and I climbed into the front seat. There was a stack of papers on the floorboard. As I sat down, my knees were up against my chin. David fired up the car. Immediately, hot air blasted out of the air conditioner right into my face. The windows were already rolled down. I tried to put my seat belt on but David snorted, "It doesn't work." All of a sudden, I wondered if I shouldn't have just called a cab.

David hit the gas pedal like he was Jeff Gordon. We fired out into the open traffic. He ran right up on the back of a big pickup truck, changed lanes and blasted his horn in disgust. He then screamed, "You stupid Okie!"

We cut through traffic like we were in a NASCAR race. Suddenly, the pickup David honked at pulled up next to us at a traffic light. The big cowboy looked down on me and showed me his middle finger.

David took off again when the light turned green. Finally we got to the car dealership. I climbed out of the car and thought about kissing the ground. "You want me to wait around?" David asked. "No, I'll be okay. You go ahead," I told him as calmly as possible.

I watched David as he pulled back onto the thoroughfare. The thought hit me that Plano, Texas probably has some of the fastest, most congestive traffic in the world. It didn't matter to David. He had to get back to work.

Start Your Own Charitable Event

"All of our dreams can come true if we have the
courage to pursue them."
--Walt Disney, animator

*Organizing a charitable event is a way to really make a
difference. It really isn't that hard to get one started. You just
have to use some vision and provide great energy.*

Make sure you have the right motivation. Don't put your
name on the line if you don't feel the enthusiasm in your heart.
Charitable events are not supposed to be about you. It doesn't
matter if it's a race, a golf tournament, or a dinner. Think long term
and get ready to plan.

Someone has to be the boss. There is an old saying that goes,
"We have too many chiefs and not enough indians." This is
especially true when people organize for an event. Someone has to
be in charge. Chaos will ensue if there isn't a strong leader.

Be consistent in your planning. There is another old saying that
always bugs me. It goes, "That program will just run itself." Let
me tell you something. Nothing runs itself. However, you can
direct the project to run itself as closely as possible. Have the
event at close to the same time every year. Start at the same time.
Stay at the same site if possible. Whatever you put on your first
event t-shirt should be your brand for years.

Have regular meetings. You now have a big responsibility to the
public. Meet regularly with others who want to help you. Early
morning meetings once a week will bond your group. The people

who are really serious will come to the meetings. The people who aren't so serious won't come. That way you will know who you can count on very quickly.

Delegate responsibility. When you know who you can trust, give them a job. People want to help. They just need direction. As the years go by, your event will grow. You better get people you can count on to help you.

Set your funding up for the long haul. Find sponsors that will come through year after year, and treat them right. Some will want to get involved and some won't. Ask them upfront for a commitment. Keep the commitment comfortable for the sponsor. Don't ask for too much. Make sure you form a bond with your sponsors and a strong base for your funding.

Find your replacement. Don't forget that it is about raising money. If you start allowing people to participate for free you are defeating the whole purpose of the event. Keep in mind that you won't always be around. Do you want your event to have legs and continue to grow through the years? If you do, find someone who can someday replace you.

Smile through it all. When the big day comes, never let them see you sweat. Hope for the best and expect the worst. If the event flops, just act like everything is wonderful. It will take years to build, but if your event has substance, your plan will work.

Texas Stadium

"Life is not measured by the number of breaths we take. It is measured by the moments that take our breath away."
--Maya Angelou, poet

In the fall of 2009 the Dallas Cowboys opened their new stadium in Arlington. For those of us that knew and loved the old Texas Stadium it was really sad. Here are a few thoughts on the original stadium with the hole in the roof.

Game Day. Most people in the country thought of Texas Stadium as the home of the Dallas Cowboys. Football fans also viewed it as one of the traditional sites of the Texas High School playoffs. There were as many as four games on a Saturday in November or December. The security guards would hold the team bus in the parking lot until they could unload the previous teams from the locker rooms. The anticipation would drive everybody crazy, but you had to wait. "The Breakfast Bowl" would start at 10:00 AM. There were many upsets in the first game, because it was a crap shoot knowing how kids would play at that time of the day. Nobody wanted to play in the nightcap, either. Many times it didn't kickoff until almost 10:00 PM.

The stadium had a great tradition. They always would print all the players a nametag to go above their locker just like the Cowboys. They did it for every team that ever visited the stadium. It was always a great thrill for the kids to walk in and see their names up in an NFL locker room.

The Weather. Texas Stadium was always hot in the summer and cold in the winter. There was no air conditioning or heating. There was also no ventilation. Of course, the fans were always protected from rain, sleet or snow, but they did have to deal with a huge temperature range.

It was different for the players and coaches on the field. I remember a game when it rained so hard that water was standing up to our ankles. You could barely see across the field. I looked up in the stands. Everyone was as dry as a bone.

The History. There were so many great games played there, and I'm not talking about the Cowboys and the Redskins. Highland Park, Southlake Carroll, Odessa Permian and Plano were just a few of the teams that often played there. The crowds swelled as the playoffs moved close to the end. In the 1977 state championship game 49,550 people watched Plano beat Port Neches-Grove.

The Stories. One playoff game we drew the nightcap on a Friday night. The game wouldn't start until about 9:30 P.M. We were having a very difficult season, and I was really not feeling much good about anything. It rained all day long, and it was torture to wait out the start of the game. It reeked like a loss.

Around noon, I was walking up to the principal's office when, like a ghost, a friend of mine walked around the corner. He startled me. "What are you doing here?" I asked him. This guy literally traveled the world in his job. "I was reading the sports page and saw you were playing tonight," he replied. "I decided to fly in to see the game."

I took him back to the field house. I told a manager to get my friend a sideline jacket. I remember the look on his face when he received a maroon raincoat with PLANO written across the back.

We pulled the game out right at the end. After we got all the players on the bus my friend offered me a ride home. There was only one problem, we couldn't find his car. Then it began to rain even harder. Texas Stadium was a big place. The stadium workers had all taken off for home. We were lost in the parking lot. It seemed like forever until we finally found his car. By then, it was close to three o'clock in the morning.

On the way home I said to my buddy, "I am so glad that you came to see us win this game." I immediately sensed disappointment from him. I asked him if something was wrong. "I didn't come to see you win," he said. "I came to be here with you in case you lost."

Fieldhouse Barbeque

"Don't wait for leaders; do it alone, person to person."
--Mother Teresa, humanitarian

Use food any time you can to rally your troops. It's a very simple leadership tool. People will respond to food, especially if you prepare it yourself. It binds people together and gives them something to talk about. It also gives them something to look forward to regarding your program.

Start cooking as a hobby. We were going through a tough losing stretch. I was looking for anything I could do to turn things around. The thought hit me about cooking for the football team. We had strict rules that we had to follow. We had to charge the kids whatever it cost for the meal. I kept it very simple and figured out how to do it very inexpensively. I usually only had to charge the kids a dollar or so to pay for everything. I provided all the labor.

I got this weird kick out of the challenge to cook for a large number of people for a low cost. I never tried to impress anybody. I bought pre-cooked meat. I heated it up to where I liked it. Then I took credit for it.

Create a brand. I made up some t-shirts with Fieldhouse Barbeque written across the front like a baseball jersey. On the bottom scroll was Plano, Texas. Then in quotation marks it said, "We keep it simple." Before I knew it, everyone wanted one of those t-shirts.

Expansion. Soon I was doing FCA meetings, track meets and even a banquet. I also cooked for some big parties at our house. Fieldhouse Barbeque developed quite a reputation, and it will be with me forever. I expanded things after I became athletic director. The cooking events got bigger and bigger, and I experimented more and more. If you are reading this book, you are probably looking for ideas on leadership. Use food more in your organization. Your people will like it. However, you will be the one who benefits the most.

Say it ain't so, Joe

"Never look down on anyone unless you are helping him up."
--Jesse Jackson

*The best stories are about the most outlandish characters.
Many times these characters are misunderstood. They are
just thrust into some weird situations. It is important to hear
people out and get to the bottom of their story. If you don't,
you could be missing out on the truth completely.*

Hear them out. No matter how bad the story is you need to listen
to the accused side of things. Never react over hearsay. Almost
everyone wants to do the right thing. Sometimes things get crazy.
When someone gets in trouble, be the person who at least listens to
both sides. Your instincts will tell you what to do.

Think the punishment through. Punish the guilty party, but
don't ban them for life. People learn from their mistakes. Always
give a kid a chance to come back the next year if you have to kick
him off the team. Examine what the punishment will do to the kid.
Don't just throw him under the bus.

Be open to showing some compassion. Early in my head
coaching career I had this wild kid on our team named Joe. His
mom was single, and she was doing everything she could to corral
him. She was working two jobs to pay the bills; therefore he was
home alone a lot. He was really a good kid at heart. I found out
later that a lot of the kids would take advantage of him. Wild
parties would break out at his house when his mom was working.
The neighbors complained all the time to the principal and me.
One night a big fight broke out in a field in Plano. It got really
ugly. Word was that Joe was right in the middle of it. I decided to
kick him off the team, but I had business to take care of first that

day. My wife and I had just had our third child, Collin. He had colic and was crying all night long. Neither Beth nor I could get any sleep. We went to the hospital to see a specialist about trying to get Collin straightened out.

When we got to the hospital the nicest lady helped us. She was an expert in dealing with infants. When it was time to leave I asked her if there was anything I could do for her. She looked at me and said, "Well, there is something you can do for me. I'm Joe's mother." She went on to explain that the football team was the only thing that she had to keep Joe in line. "Coach," she said. "If you kick him off the team, I don't know what will happen."

I kept him around. I decided that at least if he was on the team I could somewhat control him. If I kicked him off the team I would have no control over him. I figured if he was that crazy then he would be a good point man on the kickoff team. It turned out that he was just that. I never had any trouble with Joe after I met his mother.

The Terminators

"Don't tell people how to do things. Tell them what you want, and they will surprise you with their ingenuity."
--George Patton, U.S. General

In sports, the leader should always be looking for new, innovative ways to juice up his program. Off-season is always critical to success. Sometimes subordinates only need an idea or a small push to do great things. Guide them in the right direction, and get out of their way.

One year during off-season, I came up with the idea of breaking our team into special groups. My original idea was to combine coaches and players into groups that normally didn't interact with each other much on a day-to-day basis. That worked well up to a point, but the project quickly evolved into coaches wanting their position players in their own group. The program worked well. However, there was one coach that took the project to another level.

Sam Shields was almost 70 years old when I hired him to coach at Plano. The first day he was with us he proclaimed he was so old, he "remembered when the Dead Sea was only sick." Sam grew up in Plano and bled maroon and white. He previously had coached at Plano for John Clark and at Plano East for Scott Phillips. After he retired from the public schools, he went to work coaching at Hardin Simmons University in Abilene.

During one summer, one of my coaches got another job. I needed a defensive ends coach who had some experience. I almost always moved one of the younger coaches onto the varsity, but this particular situation was different. I didn't really have the person I needed ready, and I wanted some more experience on the staff. I met Sam the first year I coached at Plano, and we were always good friends. His son, Sammy, coached for us when we won the state championship in 1994. I knew Sam had grandkids in the Plano area, so I used that as my main recruiting tool to get him to come back and coach at Plano.

I encouraged our coaches to give their group a name. I wanted them to print up some t-shirts and have some fun. We made it really competitive between the groups in off-season. As the spring wound down, all the groups fizzled out but one. The one that had legs was Sam's group. He named them "The Terminators." They were almost all defensive ends, but any other kid on the team who wanted to be in their group was welcome.

In his first meeting with the Terminators, Sam told them his favorite story. A lion was walking across a field one day. He suddenly saw a big bull down the way. He ran over and jumped the bull. He ate every bit of the bull, all the way down to the bones. After he was finished, the lion decided to let out a long roar. Across the way, a hunter heard the lion's howl. He walked up within range, set his telescope, and shot the lion dead. Sam said that the moral of the story was that if you are full of bull, you better keep your mouth shut.

He also always said that every person has two wolves in his heart. One wolf was friendly and encouraging. The other wolf was angry and mean. Sam said it was up to us to decide which wolf we would feed.

With Sam around things got a lot easier for me as the head coach. If I needed something done around the campus, the Terminators were ready to do it. After practice when equipment was all over the field, I could count on the Terminators to get everything to the storage shed. They developed quite a reputation around the entire school and even the city. They had so much pride. Sam got the older kids in the group to take ownership of the younger kids.

Everybody that has ever met Sam Shields knows that he is a very interesting character. From the start he amazed the kids with physical tricks. For example, he could torque his body upside down and hold himself off the ground. It was an amazing trick that

I never understood how he could do. As soon as he arrived, we bought an indoor blocking sled for the weight room. Sam was so fired up about it that he demonstrated to all the kids how to use it. He ended up tearing his rotator cuff and had to have surgery.

Sam would get up at a ridiculous hour every morning, like 3:00 A.M., to work out. He would tell us about it later in the day very casually. "Well," he would say, "I ran my 4 miles this morning, lifted and still had time to do 1,000 sit-ups before school started." Everybody was a little astonished, but few ever doubted him. He was an old marine. He told us he would go to Iraq right now if the government would let him. No one doubted him on that for sure.

During this time, my middle son, Beau, was coming up through our program. When he was younger, Beau really wasn't very fast or athletic. My wife and I never really worried about it. When it came time for him to come to the senior high at Plano our coaches didn't really know what position was best for him. We finally decided to put him at defensive end. I told Sam, "See if you can make a player out of him."

Sam Shields always treated every player the same. He loved all of them. So obviously, Beau and Sam became very close. One night we played a junior varsity game in which I thought Beau was pretty bad. When we got back to the coaches locker room deep in the bowels of the Plano Senior High field house, I confronted Sam. It was just the two of us. "Sam," I said. "don't play Beau just because he is my kid. I thought he was terrible out there tonight. You put those other kids in there." It was just the two of us, and things got pretty heated. Sam took exception to my opinion. "He is the best we have on the JV," he told me, "and on top of that, if you think you are tough enough, we can just settle this right now." I knew he was talking about a throw down right there in the locker room. I really didn't want to get into a fistfight with a 70 year old guy. People who know me know I don't back down very easily, but I did that time.

After that, I didn't coach Beau much. I just let Sam coach him. The next spring Beau grew three inches and became an outstanding player. He went on to get a football scholarship. Sam and I went out together at Plano. Our last game was against the eventual state champion, Euless Trinity Trojans. By the time we reached the state semi-final game against Trinity we had lost both Beau and our other defensive end, Cameron Kistler, to injuries. Trinity had a huge offensive line and was the most physical team in the state. The Terminators circled the wagons. Both of their starters were out of the game. They threw everything they had into every meeting, every practice, and every play in the game. Beau and Kistler were just like assistant coaches. They also were unbelievable cheerleaders. Our team played valiantly, but we lost in double overtime.

After the game, I moved to my full time duties as the district athletic director. Sam decided to go back to Hardin Simmons. We all learned a lot from The Terminators, but we learned a lot more from Sam Shields.

Momentum = Confidence

"In the decisive set, confidence is the difference."
--Chris Evert, tennis player

Confidence is critical to success. It flows up and down as time goes by. If you understand confidence you might be able to control it. At the very least you should make an effort to try to factor it into your program.

Understand momentum and confidence. You hear it all the time when you are watching games on TV. "The momentum has suddenly changed," the play by play guy tells us. The reason the momentum has changed is because one team has gotten a sudden confidence boost. The synergy is different. The aggressed suddenly becomes the aggressor.

Create momentum changers. Great leaders are always looking for ways to change momentum. How do they do it? They look for ways to change the confidence of their team. It could be a trick play. It could be a play that the coach knows will work. It could also involve specific personnel. It also could be something that occurs during the week in preparation for the game. A good coach is always looking for some kind of a confidence booster. It should also be pointed out that a team can be too confident. In that situation, the coach might want to work the other way and humble his team.

Build on easy tasks. Teach kids to gather their homework and always start with the easiest subject first. That will build confidence. Then go to the next hardest task. Soon their confidence will turn into momentum. Always remember that most things are not as difficult as you think they will be to finish. Ben Franklin said it best, "To start is to be half finished."

Strong coaches exude confidence. It is very important to end every day on a positive note. Tell your players and coaches that you never have a bad practice. Some practices are just better than others. Make sure at the end of practice you give the kids something positive to take home.

The Thickest Skin in Town

"Nobody can make you feel inferior without your consent."
--Eleanor Roosevelt

Leaders are always going to be under the microscope. If you are going to take on a leadership role, you better get ready for the criticism. It hurts. Don't let anyone tell you that it doesn't. You just have to realize that criticism and pressure come with the job.

Understand human nature. I will tell you one thing I remember about the coaching business. If you get ten or twelve head coaches together, the conversation will always get around to the same subject. Every coach will have stories about parents who turned on them because their child didn't get an athletic scholarship. The parents said the coach didn't do enough to help. If you ever become a head coach, you will probably have this problem. First, you must realize that it is very difficult for parents to be objective about their own kids. It just goes against human nature. I have seen great people at their absolute worst when it comes to their kids. You cannot hold a grudge against a kid or a parent. You must let it go, and let it slide off your shoulders. That is the best advice I can give any coach. Holding a grudge is bad for business.

Realize that word travels fast. In this age of the internet and rapid communication, word travels really fast. If the coach ever lowers his standards and speaks negatively about anyone or uses profanity when dealing with a parent, get ready for disaster. Just don't go there. Be professional, courteous and stern. Take pride as a coach to have the thickest skin in town. There is a time to stand up and fight, but it usually isn't the best thing to do. *Never let em see you sweat.* Before the season even starts, address the issue. Have a plan about how you will handle the criticism. Take the blame for what goes wrong. Keep everything above board, and get back to work.

No excuses but lots of reasons. Don't make excuses for failure. Point the finger at yourself first and always point out the positives. However, you have to look at the reasons you failed. What went wrong? Why didn't it work? What can we do to fix it? Break down the positives and the negatives, and put it all on paper. Look at things as objectively as you can. Talk about what you need to do to get better. If you search hard enough for answers, you will find them.

Hope for the Best.
Prepare for the Worst.

"Success seems to be largely a matter of hanging on after others
have let go."
--William Feather, publisher

*If you are planning on being a high achiever, you better start
learning to deal with pressure. It comes with the territory.
Many a leader has succumbed to the daily pressure cooker.
There are ways to effectively deal with stress, problems and
high expectations.*

Recognize the pressure and respond to it. Putting your head in
the sand and dodging heat is the worst thing you can do. Break
down why you are under the gun and deal with it directly. It's
always a good idea to write it down very simply and clearly.
Always hope for the best, and prepare for the worst. If you do that,
you should be ready for almost anything.

Attack the biggest problem. Spend an entire day focusing on
your biggest problem. Find any solution you can to fix it. Go on
the offensive. Don't let other people dictate to you.

Be physical. The older I get the more I understand physical
conditioning. Everybody knows that exercise helps people deal
with stress. Plus, if you are in great shape it will help you mentally
and emotionally. Your self image is critical to helping you deal
with tough times.

Get dirty. The biggest asset you have is yourself. Don't delegate
that away. Pick the task that you love the most and execute it

yourself. Get involved in the basic operation. Call the plays. Don't farm all the decisions out to someone else.

Evaluate yourself and your program. Look at what you are doing well and what you are doing poorly. Be objective. You can't make the tough call if you don't know what the exact problem is. Attack pressure! Don't succumb to it.

The Plano Basics

"There are only two options regarding commitment.
You are either in or you are out."
--Pat Riley, basketball coach

*There are different kinds of traditions. Most of the time,
tradition is stirred by a yearning from a coach or a player. An
idea or a vision provides the motivation. Change usually is
slow, but sometimes things can happen really fast.*

Keep it simple. We didn't allow facial hair on any of the coaches
or the players. I don't know how many kids I taught to shave
while I was the coach at Plano. Many of them just didn't know
how. After I told them how to shave, they usually seemed to take a
lot of pride in it.

We also didn't allow any earrings. We were one of the few
athletic departments that made a stand on the issue. The coaches
were instructed to be cool about it. We just asked the player to
take the earring out if he was wearing one. If we continued to have
a problem, we simply told him that he had to make a choice. He
either chose the earring or the sport.

We also had a hair code. Ironically enough, the hair code was
the easiest rule to enforce. There just weren't many kids who wore
their hair long.

Teach proper respect. We didn't stop with the dress code. It was
stressed that the players respond to the coach with either a "Yes,
Sir" or "No, Sir." We made a big point that the players were to
look the coaches in the eye when there was any conversation. We
tried to make it a habit for the players and the coaches.

I always responded to any player the same way I asked them to
respond to me. I always said, "Yes, Sir" or "No, Sir" to anyone,

regardless of his age. It wasn't anything to me to say "Yes, Sir" to a ten year old kid in football camp.

It helps with the coaches. We didn't have to worry about the appearance of any of our coaches. They knew the rules, because they had to enforce them. We had people who complained, but they were in the minority. We also had coaches come and go that just didn't believe in what we were doing. That was okay. They could coach somewhere else.

John Wooden, the great UCLA coach, had the same kind of rules. One year Bill Walton decided to challenge Coach Wooden. Walton told Coach Wooden that it was against his principles to shave and get a haircut. Coach Wooden agreed. He said, "Bill, I understand your principles. We are really going to miss you."

Coach Wooden went back to practice. Walton jumped on his bicycle and pedaled as fast as he could to the closest barbershop.

Tradition counts. When I was playing football in college, I kept noticing how happy and excited guys were who went into the coaching business. I realized that coaching was a good way to go. I remember a friend of mine telling me how he got a job. He wrote a cover letter and addressed it to the head coach. He got a map of the state of Oklahoma and put 100 letters in the mail. Then he waited for responses. That sounded like a good idea to me. I did the same thing, but I sent all my letters to Texas. Only two coaches responded. One guy was from Terrell, Texas. His name was Mike Bailey. He really wanted me to come to Terrell. The other coach who responded was from Plano. His name was Tommy Kimbrough. I decided on Plano mainly because of Coach Kimbrough. Plano also had what I wanted. It was a big 5A school district north of Dallas. I called Coach Bailey and told him I was going to work for Plano. Ironically enough, a few years later he came to Plano East as the head coach. I think I would have ended up in Plano anyway.

Coach Kimbrough was the hardest working man I was ever around. I was around some hard working men, too. He was totally committed to what he was doing. I always felt that was his biggest strength. He knew how to block everything out that wasn't important, and he focused on the important issues.

I knew some really good coaches in Oklahoma, but Coach Kimbrough was different. He knew what he wanted, and he was disciplined. He was a person of faith. His family was everything to him, and he wanted to coach kids and win football games.

There was no cussing or nonsense around the field house. We had a lot of fun, but it was all above board. I learned that you could eliminate foul language and cheap shots and still have a good time. We worked some really long hours. That was back in the day of the 16 millimeter film. You had to turn the lights off in the room to see the picture. It was really dark in there. It was a great place for a coach to tell a dirty joke or say something rude. But it didn't happen. Coach Kimbrough set such a high standard that everybody knew not to act that way. I remember my wife bringing the kids into the back of the room late on a Saturday afternoon. She never had to worry about a thing that was said.

He sent me over to see the athletic director, John Clark. Coach Clark had been the coach at Plano before Coach Kimbrough. People I met in town had already told me that Coach Clark was an even better coach than Coach Kimbrough. He only lost a handful of games during the eleven years he was the head coach. He told me what he expected of coaches. It was simple and direct. He was extremely impressive.

Both Coach Clark and Coach Kimbrough ran things their way. They both believed in core values, hard work and spirit. After a few years, Coach Clark retired and Coach Kimbrough became the athletic director. I became the head coach. Most of the principles I express in this book come from their influence.

In 1994, we beat Odessa Permian in the state semi-finals. It would be the second straight trip to the championship game for the Wildcats. The state game is always on TV in Texas. We had ruined our white jerseys a few weeks before while playing on a muddy field. I was the one to bring up the idea to buy new jerseys and put the kids' names on the back. There was only one dissenter, Jaydon McCullough, who eventually became my replacement. He voted no. He didn't think it was appropriate for Plano. We went ahead with it anyway.

The booster club president handled it with great skill. None of the players ever found out about what we were up to. However, Coach Kimbrough did find out about it. I should have told him. However, the plan was in place. It was too late.

The *Dallas Morning News* wanted to do a story on the three of us and the Plano tradition. We met on Thursday morning at Clark Stadium. It was raining. I mean it was really raining. We met with the photographer and the writer inside the home locker room. After all the pictures, we had to wait out the rain to get to our cars. You could cut the tension with a knife. I knew I had to tell Coach Clark everything about the jerseys.

As we were standing at the doorway watching the driving rain, I asked Coach Kimbrough, "Coach, have you told Coach Clark about the jerseys?" He just looked at me. "No," he said. "I was going to let you tell him." I looked at Coach Clark. "Well, Coach," I said. "we bought new jerseys for the state game, and we put the kids' names on the back."

It got really quiet, and then Coach Clark bailed me out. "Well, if you think it will help you win, I guess it's okay." It was like taking a thousand pounds of weight off my back.

The next day, we drove to College Station to play Katy. It was still rainy and cold. We worked on the jerseys all night. On Saturday morning, we pulled up to the locker room gates at Kyle Field. Everything was ready inside. The players' jerseys were hung in place.

I decided to stay outside. The story goes that John Spae, one of our best players, walked in first. He saw the jerseys hanging in the lockers. "I can't believe A&M didn't take their stuff down," he said. Suddenly, he realized that it was his jersey with his name. A giant roar went up in the locker room.

An announcer named Craig Way was doing the game on TV. He came up to me on the field before the game. "I can't believe you had the guts to do that," he said.

It was really windy and cold during the game. We only threw one pass, and it was incomplete. We had lost to Converse Judson in the championship game the year before. We didn't handle the TV timeouts well in that game. This year we were ready. We were timing the commercial minutes during the first half. Late in the second quarter Katy was driving. The coaches in the press box told me that there were still six minutes of TV commercials left. I waited until they walked to the line of scrimmage, and I called timeout. It was the smartest thing I did all day. It seemed like an eternity until we started playing again. Katy self destructed.

We started the fourth quarter with a 28-0 lead. All of a sudden, two of our reserve players came up to me and said, "Coach, we have to go to the bathroom." I was a little perturbed, but I let them go. What happened next became Texas High School football history. The two players walked into the locker room and found two crooks going through our players' belongings. As soon as they saw our players, the crooks bolted for the door. The two football players chased them right out the door and onto the street outside the stadium.

You have to understand that the press box was on the other side of the stadium from our locker room. Everybody up there watched two football players in full pads chasing two crooks on foot. The players caught them and pounced on them. Then they realized that they had to get back to the game.

I had no idea any of this was happening. We won the game, and the media was all over me. My wife ran over to me, and I gave her one of those token hugs you give someone when you are really busy. That was the dumbest thing I did all day. That put me in the dog house for a month. All the TV people wanted to know about was the chase. I didn't even know what they were talking about.

Late that night we were back in Plano watching the news. The big story was about two football players chasing down crooks at the state championship game. Nobody said anything about Plano putting names on the back of their jerseys.

CHAPTER 2
Leadership

60% players	40% coaches

From the Outside Looking In

"One of the true tests of leadership is to recognize a problem before it becomes an emergency." --Arnold Glasow, humorist

It is easy to criticize when you are on the outside looking in. There isn't any pressure, and everything looks easy. It is another matter when you are on the inside looking out. For leaders, sometimes it seems you are at the bottom of a silo. But think it through. Doesn't it make sense to sometimes use suggestions from someone who is looking at your program from a more objective point of view?

Strong leaders seek advice. They don't always use the advice, but they do seek it out. Smart people know what they don't know. When you are in the day to day struggle, it can be difficult to see your weaknesses. If you, as the leader, can find a person who knows what he is talking about, you are foolish not to listen to him. This type of rational thinking goes against human nature. People don't like to be criticized. They especially don't like seeking out a criticizer.

Your ego can handle it if you really want to win. The bottom line is simple. You are searching and working to be at your best. If an outside critic can help you, use him. This person doesn't need to come to staff meetings, and he should only communicate with you personally. He should be someone who can use tact, but that isn't a necessity. This is a project you should work on long term. You should have regular meetings with this mentor. You should give him the agenda you want him to use. Now that I have been out of coaching for a while I understand this concept well. When I was coaching, I wasn't so fired up about an idea like this.

Ask for help about details. Ask your mentor to evaluate anything and everything. Start with the perception of your team. What kind of image do we have? Ask all kinds of questions. Be thick skinned and get the feedback you need. This relationship has to be special. It's like father and son. You don't have to do everything your mentor suggests, but you do need to listen. If you really want to win, give it a try.

Everybody Needs a Library

"The faintest ink is better than the best memory."
--Chinese proverb

The average couple will change residences 3 or 4 times during a long marriage. As the years fly by it gets more and more difficult to keep up with important personal belongings. Don't hesitate about becoming the family historian. To make it fun, give it a personal touch.

Be on the lookout for a place and a library unit. Find a suitable place in your place of residence. It can be large or small, but it needs to be convenient. Place your library where you have easy access and room to grow. Keep it simple. You can find a shelving unit, new or used, almost anywhere. Start with one shelf if you have to. You can upgrade later. Just make sure you can get to your material easily and enjoyably.

Make books your central component. If you have never kept up with books this is your opportunity. You have them around; you just might not realize it. People you love have books and materials that are important to them. Place books strategically. You will be surprised at what you start collecting.

Keep track of documents. Insurance papers, wills, warranties and family documents are all examples of valuable papers that people often cannot find. Your originals should be in a fireproof place, but your library should be your backup. Pictures and videos are also examples of items that are close to the heart but often are lost in the shuffle of life.

Develop an eye for collectibles. You will be surprised how quickly you will pick up books and other items that have value. The value could be financial or personal. It will also put heart into your library.

Where are your trophies and certifications? A very upset couple came into my office to complain about a coach. I knew going in they had a very valid point to their argument. I had only been the athletic director for a short time. They weren't mad at me. They were mad at one of our coaches. I tried to step into the conversation. I made a statement about the behavior of people. The mom jumped all over some point I made. "What kind of education do you have to make a statement like that?" I looked around the room. I didn't have anything on any wall. I had plenty of education to make the statement, I just had no proof. I went home that night and rounded up all my diplomas and certifications. I had everything framed. Then I put them in the library in my office. I made sure that never happened again.

Rev Up Your Meetings

"Every leader needs to make sure that everybody in his
organization knows his three main goals."
--Jeffrey Immelt, businessman

*Most professional people have the same attitude toward a
meeting. They are interested if the meeting has substance and
isn't a waste of time. However, many leaders aren't trained on
how to conduct strong, productive meetings. Here are a few
tips on how to get the most out of a short get together.*

Plan the big picture. Strong achievers are always looking at the
big picture. Never meet just to meet. Always have an agenda that
includes short term, medium term, and long term issues. Organize
the agenda on paper and pass it out to your people.

Start on time and move quickly. Don't worry about everybody
being present to start a meeting. Start when you told everyone you
would start. People have things to do. Sometimes they run a little
late. When it becomes a big deal to you about tardiness, address
it immediately. People don't like coming in late. Starting on time
consistently usually takes care of tardiness.

Study the meeting room. The leader should pay attention to the
room where the meeting takes place. He also should study where
the chairs, tables, and audio-visual equipment are set. Change
things around so the meeting room is most conducive to maximum
effectiveness. Don't be afraid to change things.

Go around the horn. A great way to involve everyone is to go
around the room and get everyone's opinion on a subject. This
involves everyone. Make sure everyone knows the rules. Do not

interrupt the speaker. Give him his brief time, and then move on to the next person.

Be selfish about major decisions. Be careful not to bring up a particular tough call. That is why you have been chosen as the leader. Some decisions will split your staff if you let them have too much input. That is why you need an agenda, and you need to stick to it.

Reinforce your 3 main objectives. Every leader should make sure that his organization knows his three basic objectives. Use meetings to reinforce exactly what you are striving to accomplish. Base your meetings around these three main goals.

Use Your Downtime Efficiently

"The discipline of writing a goal down on paper is the first step toward making it happen."
--Lee Iacocca, business executive

Rest and recreation are critical to both the mind and the body. Many great ideas, solutions, and plans have been created while people are resting or just killing time. There is a fine line between work and play. Employees should not be under pressure to think about their jobs 24/7. However, there are a few things you can do to use your downtime more efficiently.

Keep paper and pen with you at all times. Play it smart and always be ready to write down a good idea. Some of your best thoughts come when you are relaxed. Don't count on your memory. It will fail you.

Take a minute to call family and friends. As time goes by many people contact their folks or friends less and less. Be the one to initiate contact. Who cares if it's their turn to call? Use downtime to communicate with people.

Create a check list. Everyone has a long "need to do" list. Downtime while waiting on a meeting is a great time to organize and prioritize your list of things to accomplish. You immediately pick up momentum and energy. Most tasks are not really that difficult to finish.

Leaders are Readers. Strong leaders are always pursuing new material to read. Reading about strong people will not only give you knowledge and insight, but it also is a tremendous motivator. It is a good practice to always have a book on hand to read. Get into a habit of reading 2-4 pages at a time. Take a break, and then read a couple more pages. Pretty soon you will have the book finished. Many people like to keep books. Others read books and discard them. One way to show leadership is to pass books on to other people. Accept the fact that if you loan someone a book, you will probably never see it again. Don't loan it out if it is valuable to you. A book can become a great gift that really means something to family, friends, or co-workers. Figure a way to stamp your name inside the book. It is a way to inexpensively personalize your relationship. The great writer, Stephen Covey, put it simply, "Leadership is influence, and influence is leadership. That is all it is and all it ever will be." You never know how a simple gift like a book can make an impact on a friend. So get a book to carry with you. Read it, and pass it on to someone else.

Start writing your own book. Writing is just talking on paper. Some people are interested in telling their story. Other people are interested in technical material. Some people have novels festering inside their hearts. The best way to get started on a book is to make an outline. Organize your outline so that all you have to do is let it flow. Many writers claim the hardest part of writing is transitioning one subject to another. Plan your thoughts so you simply change the subject and keep moving. You might not be able to write much during downtime, but you certainly can plan how you will write when you have more time. And remember, you don't write a book. You re-write it over and over until you get it right.

Work on your game. It might be hard to practice your golf swing in an airline terminal. However, you can plan on how to improve it. Whatever sport or activity you enjoy, it is a lot more fun if you are good at it. Break down and examine how you are practicing. What can you do to get better? Write down a plan. Be specific. Be more analytical about yourself. Make yourself a schedule. Figure out how to hit the ball straight. In the game of golf, distance is fun, but accuracy is priceless.

Create the Environment

"Be a yardstick of quality. Some people are not used to an environment where excellence is expected."
--Steve Jobs, Apple co-founder

If the leader of an organization can create an environment where his people enjoy coming to work, he will be successful. That doesn't mean that he has to be a pushover in the workplace. It goes much deeper than that. People need and want structure and organization. More importantly, they want a vision of the future.

Make sure you know the direction your team is heading. Here were my three main objectives when I was an athletic director. First, do everything with integrity. That was the most important thing for any coach, player or team. The second goal was to win. I wanted to teach the kids to plan, prepare, practice, work, and execute. We also wanted to teach them how to conduct themselves whether they won or lost. Third, I wanted to balance the operating budget of the athletic department. I felt that our organization owed it to the school district and the community. It was a daunting task, but it wasn't impossible. All the coaches in the school district knew these three goals. It kept us focused as a team.

Make sure everyone knows his role. Spell out responsibility on paper to everyone involved. That doesn't mean people can't go the extra mile. It just creates a chain of command. Answer questions that have never been asked. Solve problems that haven't come up yet. Make sure everyone knows his role.

Encourage people to think and act. If you hire someone, you better trust them to make solid decisions. Leaders that micromanage often have a lot of turnover in personnel. In general, people are smart. They know what to do. There is always a time to bump a decision up to the next level, but most of the time your people can get the job done.

Planning and organization are the key. The boss needs to be the guy who has the least work to do. That way he can always be thinking about the future. The leader is the key person who sets the plan, organizes what he wants, and evaluates how things work. If the boss is constantly bogged down, it is difficult to plan the direction of the team.

Create ownership. The mark of a strong leader is that everything keeps functioning while he is away. You do that by creating ownership in your people. Many leaders have this backward. They are paranoid about letting someone else make a decision. They want total control. It takes talent and skill to run a team. You have to study it, and you have to develop it.

Deal in the truth. Problem solvers don't wait to act. The worst thing a leader can do is to keep putting a problem aside. Procrastination is the enemy. Pick up the phone and address problems immediately. You don't necessarily have to make a decision, but you do need to address the issue. If an employee is out of line, address it. Don't wait. The problem will fester and grow. Make sure everyone knows your style, what you want to do and how you will tackle issues.

Take Pride in being Mentally Tough

"You may be disappointed if you fail, but you are doomed if you don't try." ---Beverly Sills, opera singer

High achievers must handle success and endure failure. Both can be difficult. Success is the fun part. Failure knocks people to their knees. How the players handle failure is usually what separates them. There is no doubt that handling tough losses is one of the keys to long term success.

Take pride in being mentally tough. We don't talk enough about mental toughness. I believe that it is a skill. You have to train yourself to be disciplined. Read about other leaders. You will find out quickly how they failed. You also will find out how they handled adversity.

It's all a game. As elementary as it sounds, treating everything like a game really works. It is also important to note that keeping score and tallying victories is also very important. You just want to win as much as you can as honorably as you can.

No matter what the game you play, you have to compete against the best to be the best. Remember, there will always be a winner and a loser. View disappointment as an event not a failure.

What can I do to improve? That is what is most important. Most people just don't talk about it enough. Ask the hard questions. Stomach the tough answers. Take pride in being mentally tough.

Sometimes you have to fake it until you make it. By that I mean that you have to show the tough exterior when it might not really be there. But when you really think about it, isn't it the biggest compliment you can give someone when you comment on how tough they are mentally?

Do as I say, Not as I do

"It's easier to be wise for others than for ourselves."
--Alexander Solzhenitsyn, author

People make mistakes. Many times they are not good examples to our young people. However, when they speak about their failures and give us advice, we should listen to them.

Cut people some slack. We all need to realize that people develop bad habits that sometimes they never conquer. Then they preach to you not to fall into the same trap. Listen to what they say. They are trying to help you. Sometimes the best example is a bad example.

People really care. As you grow older, things become much more clear to you. There is an old saying that goes like this, "If I knew then what I know now, I would have done things much differently." People will often tell you about the hard knocks they have suffered. It is okay for someone else to make mistakes for you.

It's a bigger issue than you. I really only have one regret about my coaching career. I was notorious for yelling at officials. I am not proud of it. I was not a good example to the young coaches. At least I admit it.

   When I became the district athletic director in Plano I didn't want my replacement, Jaydon McCullough, to emulate my behavior towards referees. I wanted him to be more patient, but I also wanted a change in perception for the Plano program. It is a classic example of "do as I say, not as I do."

The last year I coached, we played all the way to Christmas. I wanted to get all the assistant coaches something personal for a present. I told the team photographer to take as many pictures of me with the other coaches as possible. When Christmas came around, I gave every coach on the staff a framed picture with the both of us in it. It was no big deal. It was just special to me.

I gave Jaydon a second framed picture. This picture was of me about to blow a gasket yelling at a referee. "This is how I do not want you to coach," I told him. You would have to talk to him, but I think I got my point across.

Balance the Workload

If you have an intense leadership position, you better think about how you will sustain your program over the long haul. The coaching business is a good example. The hours are long. The work is tedious, and the situations are volatile. You need a plan to keep your people fresh, productive and motivated.

Plan the grind. If you work long hours, the least you can do for your employees is to make the hours consistent. When I first started coaching, our staff never knew when we would be finished at night. Sometimes it was early. Sometimes it was late. A couple of years after I became the head coach, I structured the work hours so they would always be consistent. It didn't matter who we played, the work hours stayed the same. The coaches knew exactly when to be at the field house, and they knew exactly when they could go home. The hours were still tough, but everyone knew exactly what was going on. It really helped morale.

Insure readiness. I was always big on readiness. In other words, I always felt we should have some sort of plan even if we didn't have a lot of time to study the situation. That took a lot of work in the off-season. The more you brainstorm about the future, the better you will be prepared for problems. Planning reduces stress. I wanted a plan for how to deal with every problem at the drop of a hat.

Push the sense of urgency. In a tense, pressure packed environment, the clock is always ticking. The leader must make sure that everyone realizes it. There is a time to relax and a time to work. If you organize your schedule, you will waste less time. When I was coaching, I rarely got upset unless I realized that we were wasting time. Wasted time is the enemy of any leader.

Promote from within. Sometimes you can't promote from within. However, if you can promote from within, it is the best way to go. You also need to give your people a way to separate from the pack. Some people don't want a lot of responsibility. They just want a job and to contribute. That's okay. You actually need both leaders and followers to balance the staff. Make it clear how to move up in your organization. The best way to do that is to ask your employees to apply for positions. That way you don't take things for granted. When you give them a new position, you better state the expectations. They either do it, or they don't do it. If they don't get it done, you have to either do a better job training them, or you have to replace them.

Pay close attention to Staff Chemistry

"Giving people self confidence is by far the most important thing that I can do. Then they will act."

--Jack Welch

Times change and so do the people who work for you. Personalities sometimes clash. Egos get hurt, and hard feelings are cemented. There are some things you can do as a leader to head off problems and create strong chemistry. If the leader lets things get out of control, he is asking for disaster.

The bar is set by the leader. Many times people are thrust into leadership roles without proper training or experience. One thing the leader can do is to set a personal high standard. The leader should not lower his standards to profanity or gossip. These are two things you can do that people will respect. If the head guy cusses and talks about other people, he is setting the standard for everyone else. Place your standards high as a leader, and it will help your program. Remember, just keep everything above board.

You can't make people like each other. However, you can demand that they get along in the workplace. There will be natural personality conflicts. However, if you are in a position to hire people individually, make sure you set the standard immediately. Make it clear about how you expect your staff to conduct themselves professionally. Employees need to stick together. If your people start arguing among themselves and criticizing each other, then you have failed as the leader. If an employee can't work under your expectations, find a way to release him.

Create an environment where people want to come to work.
One of the best signs of a strong leader is when employees really like their work environment. That doesn't mean to create a party atmosphere. That does mean to make your objectives clear and your expectations high. You can create an atmosphere of respect, work ethic and pride. It is important for the boss to have a relationship with every single employee. He should also have a relationship with the team in general. Fun is a great motivator. Try to enjoy yourself along the way. Life is too short.

Find Your System

"Life is like a 10 speed bicycle. Most of us have gears
we never use."
--Charles Schultz, cartoonist

*People often complain about the same daily schedule.
Sometimes the routine can get boring. However, change your
normal routine for a couple of days. You will find that you will
probably go back to your old ways. The point is this: your
normal daily routine is critical to your success at anything.
Everyone is different and has a different schedule, but a little
tweaking here and there can make a big difference.*

Break it down. I have heard for years that if you want to spend
less money you need to write down everything you spend on paper.
If you want to lose weight, write down what you eat every day.
You will begin to see a pattern to your schedule. Then it is up to
you to try to change it.

Don't make your life miserable. Here is a common theme about
exercise. Someone decides to go on an exercise program. He
figures he should get up at 6:00 A.M. every day to exercise. The
problem is that he hasn't seen six A.M. in years. Most likely he is
doomed to fail.

There is nothing wrong with making change friendly. Find the
easiest way to change, not the hardest. You will have a much
better chance for success.

Figure out your body clock. Match your schedule to your
natural body clock. Sure, you will have to make adjustments
because of work, the kids or whatever else, but you will have a
much better chance of winning if you follow your own natural

tendencies. Don't try morning exercise if you hate getting up early. Find a time when you feel awake and strong.

Make your own schedule. I heard Mary Kay Ash tell her story once in Dallas. She said she thought the key to her success was simple. Every night before she went to bed she would write down six things to get done the next day. She focused on those six objectives until completion. Someone from the audience asked her for an example. She responded, "Oh well, one example would be to take out the trash." Everyone laughed, but think about it. Simple is good. Doing something easy creates momentum to start getting things accomplished. What do you really want to change? Focus on simple things and success will follow.

0 and 10

"Pain is temporary; quitting lasts forever."
--Lance Armstrong

I was once the head coach of a team that didn't win a game all year in Texas varsity high school football. Our staff had to figure out how to dig out of a deep hole. Here is how we did it.

Train, train, and train some more. Our staff instituted Wednesday night clinic sessions. Every Wednesday night session was broken into three parts. We kept the start and end times punctual to the minute. That way everyone knew exactly what was going on. People could come in and out of the meetings with confidence.

The first session always dealt with faith, fellowship and team building. It was usually the lowest attended session, but it was always my favorite. We touched on a lot of important issues in the first session. Critical decisions about our team's direction were made when a lot people didn't even realize it.

The second and third sessions focused on serious football strategy and scheme. All of our position coaches presented, but we did have some guest speakers. New ideas developed. Tough questions about how and why we did things were asked. We emphasized a tougher work ethic. We created stronger study habits. We really grew as a staff.

Make everything a game. We changed our philosophy about how we coached. Our staff wanted the highlight of every player's day to be football practice. That didn't mean practice wasn't tough. We just made everything tough and fun. We created all kinds of competition during off-season. We developed ways for the kids to earn recognition. Instead of having a spring game, we had four spring games. We split into competitive teams. We turned on the scoreboard and kept score. It was as close as we could get to a real game. Every kid on our team got to experience four Friday night games. The competition was tremendous.

The main focus became execution. We still worked long, tough hours preparing game plans on weekends. However, we made a commitment to focusing more on the execution of every single play. If we couldn't execute a play, we dropped it. It forced us to simplify, but we still had an excellent scheme. Simplicity massaged confidence. Confidence created momentum. We conditioned our players hard, but we didn't hit as much in practice. We focused on assignment, technique, effort, and execution. We invested in more classroom time with the players. We also instituted a planned out motivation series that focused on long term success. By Friday night, our guys couldn't wait to play.

Create a Sense of Urgency

"No great performance ever came from holding back."
--Don Greene, performance coach

One of the smartest things a coach can do for his team is to instill a sense of urgency. It is human nature for people to become complacent. They just don't realize how fast the clock is ticking.

Use fear as a motivator. Several of the best coaches used fear as one of their biggest motivators. I heard Jimmy Johnson say once that he didn't want anyone on his team, players or coaches, to feel too comfortable about anything. Johnson was famous for creating a crisis if things got too comfortable. He would find something that would rile everyone up and get them nervous. One year the Dallas Cowboys clinched a playoff spot early in the season. After a poorly played win, Johnson cut a popular player. The player had been late for a meeting during the week. Then he played poorly in the game. It caused quite a stir on the team, but things picked up around the practice field. A strong leader walks a tightrope on this issue.

Gauge the mood of your team. If you feel things are just too comfortable, change the mood. The easiest way to do that is to get riled up in practice or in meetings. Remember, the great leaders are great actors, too. You can even tell your assistants before practice what you are getting ready to do if you want.

There is an old saying in the coaching business. "Be tough on the players when things are going well. Be easy on them when times are tough." I think you should trust your instincts about what to do and when to do it. Great leaders just know.

Keep it simple. Remember the 70-30 split theory. It is 70% the players and 30% the coaches. If you get too complicated, you risk making mistakes. Keep it simple and pound the details into your team.

Seek out the defenders. One of my oldest tricks was to find a coach who would defend a particular kid. We would get deep into personnel meetings. We would get to some kid that I thought should be getting more playing time. I would start ripping on the kid. I would say he didn't have the talent or that he wouldn't hustle. I knew that some coach on the staff would almost always come to the kid's defense. As soon as that happened, I would change the kid's position to the coach who took up for him. It worked almost every time.

Address the situation. The most important thing to do is to go over all the ramifications with your team about what could happen at the game. The head coach should address everything from the weather at kickoff to travel arrangements. State to the team exactly what the plan is to get home after the game. Make sure they all understand where you stand if you lose or if you win the game. If you still are looking for ways to motivate the players, look to the history books on your team. There is a good chance, especially at the end of the season, to come up with something to catch their attention.

Think it All the Way Through

"Success covers a multitude of blunders."
--George Bernard Shaw, playwright

*It can be really easy to get carried away with a great idea.
When high achievers see a vision they often want to take the
ball and run with it. However, hasty decisions can get you in
trouble and take the fun out of everything. Be careful when a
brainstorm comes along. It is smart to make sure you follow
a few rules.*

Get feedback from your staff. Almost certainly, you will have
someone in your office that will play the Devil's Advocate. Get
your staff together and tell them your idea. Go around the horn,
and hear everyone out. Get as much feedback as you possibly can
about your idea.

Explore the risks. Determine quickly if there is a downside and
what could go wrong. Be prepared for the whole thing to blow up
in your face.

Think it through. Imagine every possible scenario. Many people
will roll their eyes at you about some of the things that **could**
happen. If it could happen, it **probably** will.

Get word to your superiors. The last year I coached at Plano was
also my first year as the district athletic director. We had a huge
game against Allen. The crowd was right at 15,000. The State Fair
of Texas had just begun. Grambling and Southern were playing
at the Cotton Bowl the next day. The Navy Seal parachute team
was going to parachute out of a plane and deliver the ball for the
coin toss before their game. They called us and asked if they could
make a trial jump at our game. I thought it was a great idea.

The big moment arrived. Sure enough, four skydivers jumped from a circling plane and landed on the field right before the opening kickoff. The crowd loved it, but I never thought to notify the Plano Police Department. When the Seals jumped, the circuit board at the police department lit up like a Christmas tree. Some citizens thought we under a terrorist attack.

I got my hands slapped a little on that one. It was a lot of fun, but I should have thought things through a little more.

Force Yourself to Learn

"Ben Franklin might have discovered electricty, but it was the guy who invented the meter who got rich."
--Earl Wilson, columnist

Learning a new skill usually takes great effort and commitment. You probably will have to really push yourself. It doesn't matter why you are learning this new skill. It does matter how you go about it. To reach your full potential, you have to get things in order.

Surrender to get help. Your first move is to check your ego at the door. If you don't understand something, you have to get some help. Stop fighting it, and start addressing the problems. Don't fight the teacher. Most people feel proud to help anyone. Ask for help, and you will get it. I have never considered myself really that good at anything. I have just always been good at getting other people to help me get things done.

Create a simple system. Plan your process, and then break it down into parts. Keep it as simple as possible. Don't go to step 2 until you have mastered step 1.

Limit your focused time. Work in 15 or 20 minute blocks of time. Give it everything you have studying this new task. Then take a 5 minute break. It will take pressure off you, and it forces you to digest information.

Create momentum. Most tasks are not nearly as difficult as you think. You just have to get started. Procrastination is the enemy. Dive in and get started. Start with the easiest part, because you will build momentum.

Just Take the Blame

There are a lot of reasons why things go wrong. However, if you are the leader of any organization, you should be the one to step up and take responsibility. Even if it isn't your fault, and many times it isn't, it is the high achiever that usually takes the fall. Here are some ways to turn negatives into positives.

Realize it is a strong symbol of leadership. I read many years ago about the great Bear Bryant. After every loss he would address the team and take all the blame for losing. Here was arguably the greatest college coach of all time, and he was taking the blame for college kids. It endeared him to his players. They knew he wasn't the only reason for the loss. It was his way of owning failure.

You get quick analysis. Another great coach I knew, Tommy Kimbrough, would take it a step further. He not only took the blame, but he would state exactly why he failed. I remember that he often blamed his play calling for a loss. Even though he was still the head coach, he was the best offensive coordinator ever. He put in unbelievable hours in preparation. No doubt, his guise as a play caller won us many a game, but when we lost, he always pointed the finger at himself.

It takes pressure off the subordinates. There is enough pressure to go around for everybody. Strong leaders realize this and take it on themselves.

Control the classroom environment. Bill Walsh, the Hall of Fame coach, always made a point in his teachings to talk about the classroom environment. He believed in an air conditioned, comfortable room where everyone could concentrate. I remember him saying, "If you have something really important to tell your players, do it in an environment where they can concentrate. Don't lecture them on the field in 90 degree heat. They can't concentrate on what you are saying." Many coaches don't realize that the time spent in the classroom is as important as practice time spent on the field.

Praise the performer. Critique the performance. Young leaders have a natural reaction to criticize the performers personally. Remember, everything can be corrected in time. Take ownership and teach, correct, and praise the effort of your subordinates.

Never berate your people. Why humiliate anyone? What good does it do for you, him or your team? If your team is failing, so are you.

Boundaries vs. Limitations

Leaders walk a fine line when it comes to motivation. It is important to set guidelines, but it is just as important to encourage people to pursue their dreams.

Never set a limitation on a dream. It is important to support people when they are passionate about a project. In the back of your mind you may be skeptical, but you should never dampen the spirit of another person's vision. This is especially true if they are really passionate. If it is a pipedream, let them be the one to see it first.

Don't kill off their hope. Just about every kid that ever plays high school sports has a dream about playing in the pros someday. Very few kids will actually make it. That doesn't mean you should be the one to dampen a young athlete's dream. You never know. He may make it someday.

You do need to set some boundaries. It's funny. People hate rules. However, rules are necessary for structure. When parenting, you must provide boundaries for your children. If the boundaries are too wide, you risk losing control. Don't worry about what rules other parents have for their kids. You need to decide what is best for your kids, but it is important that you also know what is going on in the culture around your family.

Have an answer for the questions. When your loved ones come to you with questions, give them answers. Trust your instincts. When you respond instinctively, it reflects what you really think. But you better beware. The key is to create an environment of trust and understanding. Work on your relationships with everyone. All you have to do is be nice and listen to them. When people know they can trust you, they will come to you for help.

Insource vs. Outsource

"Innovation distinguishes between being a leader or a follower."
--Steve Jobs

For years I have watched young coaches work their way up to the head coaching position. I have seen one trend that has always bothered me. Many people spend years striving to get to a leadership position. When they get there, they delegate all the decisions. I don't understand that. The reason a person is named head coach is because he was supposed to be the best coach. In any endeavor, make sure you use your biggest asset, yourself. There are times to go out and get help, but often you are better off to do it yourself.

Realize that the program revolves around you. Don't delegate decisions that will affect your team's future. That is why you are the leader. It is okay to hear other's opinions. As a matter of fact, I recommend it. However, you need to make the hard decisions. If an assistant doesn't believe in the direction you are going, he needs to move on to another job.

Outsource when you need information. If you are in trouble and need help, you need to outsource. When there are problems you cannot figure out how to fix, outsource. When you are seeking new direction, outsource. There are times when it is vital to go to another source for help. Just don't run for help every time a problem arises. First, try to solve it yourself.

Look for better ways to do things. Be the guy to push the envelope on the program. How can we do things better? How can we be more efficient? Those are the questions strong leaders ask. Just remember that it is important to be open to change, but it is more important to change slowly.

The leader needs to be the number one trainer. If you take on any leadership position, you better take on the role of the number one trainer. Teaching your troops how you want things done is more important than anything. It will give your program substance and staying power. Take pride in your ability to teach, to communicate and to motivate. Don't worry about what people think. You can evaluate things later. The important thing is to decide exactly what you want taught. Then you need to make a schedule of when you will teach it to them.

Make the tough calls. I always felt when I was coaching that when the game was on the line I wanted to be the one to make the tough call. If you delegate all your authority you can't do this. Remember, all the players, coaches and fans are watching. If the game is on the line and you don't have a vehicle to be the decision maker, you will lose credibility as the leader.

How to Teach Discipline

"The only one who can beat me is me."
--Michael Johnson, track athlete

Instilling discipline into your team isn't easy. However, it can be done. The first step is easy. Talk about it with your staff, and talk about it with your team. Define it for them. Webster's dictionary defines discipline as "to train or develop by instruction and to exercise in self control." It starts with understanding what discipline means. You can expand it from there.

Look at discipline from a broad point of view. There is discipline on the field and discipline off the field. You must have both. Explain to your team that you can have fun, be loose and still be disciplined. A strong leader will state exactly what his expectations are for the program. Most people don't like to have a lot of rules. However, if you don't have rules, how do people know your expectations? State your objectives very clearly to your team. Don't pin yourself into a corner on what you will do when you punish the rule breakers. Just make sure you are consistent. Everybody makes mistakes. Don't be so rigid that you ask for trouble. Just have high expectations and follow through on punishment if rules are broken. Always deal in the truth. Don't make excuses and exceptions. You will find as a leader that things will be much easier in the long run if you have high expectations and develop discipline in your program.

Discipline on the field is another matter. Throughout this book I have talked about planning. As the leader, you must have the discipline to formulate the plan, and then you must have the discipline to follow through with the plan. It's really pretty simple.

Make a plan, and follow through with it. The head guy must be the chief example. Lead by action. If your team is fumbling too much, address the issue. Then institute a drill to enforce it. Talk about it every day. Emphasize the proper technique to handle the ball. Break it down into statistics after each game or even after each practice. I bet you will cut down on fumbles.

Talk about discipline every day. I could go on and on about how to instill discipline. However, I really believe the best way to create discipline is to do the following: Make a plan, explain it to the people in your program every day, and then follow through with it. It's as simple as that. People who communicate what they want usually get it.

Don't Underestimate
Your Influence

"I can live two months on a good compliment."
--Mark Twain

Be sure that you are creating the image you want when you are around kids. You never know what they are picking up from you.

Watch your language. Do everything you can to strike profane words out of your vocabulary. Kids pick up on it quickly. They think it's cool when it really isn't. Don't be the reason they choose to cuss.

Always take the High Road. Kids will pick up your moral compass. Make sure you are honest and emphasize character. Stress to kids that our country really operates on the honor system. Also stress to them that no person is perfect, including you. When you make a mistake, make sure you admit it.

Realize there is a bigger picture. My grandfather, Barney Brence, had a huge impact on me. When I was a kid, he used to pick me up and take me to our farm almost every day. On the way to the farm he was always the nicest guy you could imagine. He would tell me story after story. However, when we got to the farm he would shut off the engine, get out of the pickup and suddenly become the meanest, orneriest guy I knew. He would rail on me all day long. When it was time to go home, he would get back in the pickup and be the nicest guy in town again.

All through my childhood I couldn't understand how a guy could change personalities like that. However, when I started coaching I understood. Guess what, I was just like him. I was the nicest, most approachable coach in the field house. However, when I jogged out to the practice field and crossed the white line, I became just like Barney.

People aren't perfect creatures. You have to take the good and the bad. Just remember the influence you have. Use it wisely.

Be Easy to Work For

"I don't know the secret to success, but I know the secret to failure is trying to please everybody." --Bill Cosby, comedian

There really is an art to being a good boss. People don't want the leader to be weak. They naturally want strong leadership. The boss walks a fine line between being demanding and being friendly. Here are some ideas on being the go to guy.

Spend time thinking about being the boss. The first step is simple. You must recognize that you are the boss. The second step is to evaluate the perception you are throwing out there. You had better study being in charge. What can you do to be better? Some bosses don't even recognize leadership skills much less talk about them. Everybody is watching you. The image you set for yourself will be followed by most of your employees.

Focus on training. There is an old trick for officers in the Army. When they first address their troops they make the statement, "I hope you like to train, because I love to train." Enthusiasm is critical, but knowledge is even more important. Your people will see through you if you are not solid and sound. Mold the organization in your image by the way you train your people. It is the key to building success.

Be open to criticism. In his book, It Doesn't Take a Hero," General Norman Schwarzkopf always asked for attack plans from his subordinates. He was very demanding of his officers. He would take all the plans that were submitted and study them. Then he would come up with his own plan. The next step would be to gather all the officers back together. He would then tell them to tear down his plan. All the criticism and study led to a final, detailed mission. But remember, he was the boss, and he made the final call. Be open to criticism, but don't necessarily give in to it if you don't feel it is warranted.

The Leadership Run

Sometimes people need some type of a project to get them out of a funk. The last game we played in 2001 was in Waco against Lufkin, Texas. Lufkin had a quarterback named Reggie McNeal. Reggie was the talk of the state. I have coached for years against some of the best of all time, and I would put Reggie up there with anybody who ever played high school football in Texas.

We went to see Lufkin play against Dallas Carter the Saturday before we played them. The game was on a Saturday afternoon in Dallas. Lufkin won the game easily, and Reggie was the star. There was one play in particular that stood out. Lufkin ran a double reverse that ended with Reggie throwing a long touchdown pass.

Our staff went back to Plano and immediately buried up trying to find a way to win. I started rationalizing in my mind that Lufkin wasn't all they were hyped up to be. I was trying to convince myself we could beat them. I made a comment to the defensive coordinator that I knew Reggie was good, but he wasn't a superstar. The defensive coordinator looked at me and said, "Coach, come in here, and let me show you something." I hadn't had time to really look closely at the video tape. The coach went straight to the double reverse pass. As I looked closer, I calculated that Reggie threw a 75 yard, line drive pass that hit the receiver on the dead run.

We threw everything we had into the game. We were in control with about 3 minutes to go. We were ahead, and we had Lufkin on the ropes. It was 4th and 18 from their 35 yard line. We make this stand, and we upset Lufkin, the number one ranked team in the state. But not so fast, Reggie took the snap, scrambled around, and ran 65 yards for the game-winning touchdown.

On the way home, I told my wife, Beth, that I probably should get out of coaching for awhile. When I became the head coach,

I said I would go 10 years as hard as I could. It had been the ten years, and I certainly had coached hard. I was tired.

However, things didn't work out that way. I applied for the job as the district athletic director and didn't get it. It was a tough loss for me, and I didn't handle it well. I was in a gray area professionally. On top of that, our staff knew that we were getting ready for a down period in football. We had been watching the younger kids. We knew it would be tough. I gathered the staff. We all made a commitment to see it through. Hey, we were good coaches and could squeeze out some wins, right?

Well, it wasn't that simple. I blame myself because of my attitude. I was right about getting out after the Lufkin game. I just really didn't have the fire I needed. On top of that, I had resentment and bitterness in my heart that really beat me down.

Here was the biggest mistake I made. I didn't surrender the problem to God. I tried to deal with it all myself without any help. The result was a five year stretch that almost did me in. We lost game after game. I made mistake after mistake. We lost every game one season. I was mad at the world. Then in a snap, it all changed.

The Plano Adult Fellowship of Christian Athlete chapter was always really strong. It was a support group for the FCA in the schools. The chapter had dwindled to nothing through the years. It had become non-existent. During the low point of my career, I stopped participating. Actually, everyone stopped participating.

We met at an old diner on the east side of Plano called *Poor Richard's* with the Dallas FCA representatives. "What has happened to the Adult Chapter?" they asked us. We really had no good answer for them. We agreed to start regular meetings again, but we had no funds to start any type of project. How would we deal with that?

I spoke up. As the head coach at Plano I had run off every type of fundraiser you could imagine. However, there was one fund raiser I had never been able to get off the ground. I always wanted to have a 5K race. So I asked everybody, "Why don't we have a race? I have always wanted to do it. I will be the chairman." With that statement, I started a comeback. Immediately, my attitude changed. We named the race *The Leadership Run,* because it was designed to raise money to send kids to leadership camps in the summer. I threw a lot of time and energy into the race. It became a big success very quickly. We had a vision about the race expanding to other FCA groups in the Dallas area to help with fundraising. The whole project turned out to be a tremendous experience.

I will say this about *The Leadership Run*. It probably saved my coaching career at Plano. It gave me a vehicle to realign my focus. The whole experience changed me. I see people all the time now who are going through the same thing I did. I'm sure glad we had that meeting at *Poor Richard's*. It changed my life forever.

Play to your Strengths

"The difference between being a hero and a coward is
just a step sideways."
--Gene Hackman, actor

Follow what comes naturally. If you are really good at
something it is probably because you really enjoy it. Everyone has
his own individual talent.

Look at the big picture. Be creative and find ways to pursue what
you really enjoy for a life long career. Sometimes things just don't
work out for you. You must have the ability to evaluate where
you stand. There comes a time to cut your losses and move on to
something else. It's painful, but it is necessary. That doesn't mean
you have to give up. You just might have to rearrange your goals
and ideas.

Procrastination is the enemy. Procrastination has killed more
dreams than anything. Be proactive. Get started and find a way.
Make a long term plan and a short term plan for your future. Don't
worry about it being the best plan. You can change it later.

Take a different view of the grind. People often complain about
the grind of their jobs. However, the truth is that the grind is your
friend. Most successful programs follow a system. The system
will carry you through the good times and the bad. You can change
the system, just don't abandon it.

Find a mentor. There is no better way to grow as a person than
to find a mentor. Everyone needs someone who is looking at his
career from the outside. It goes against human nature to take

criticism, but it is necessary for you to reach your full potential. Find someone who cares about you and listen to him.

Decide to win. Deciding to be successful and win isn't as hard as most people think. It is simply a choice the individual makes. Try a little bit harder. Study a little bit more. Don't be afraid to get into the arena and win.

Be strong enough to walk away. You must be strong enough as a person to walk away from negative people and negative environments. You know what is best for you more than anyone else.

Have a Little Humble Pie

We all know that confidence is very important. However, arrogance is always a loser. Figure out how to keep your personality in order by humbling yourself.

Never demean anyone's success. The most boorish attitude of all is to belittle someone else when they are successful. People will remember you if you complement them or tell them they did a good job. Be the person who makes the effort to be positive and recognize success.

Pay attention to your better half. One time we were in a big playoff game in Huntsville, Texas. During pre-game, I was pacing all over the field. All of a sudden, I see a Plano cheerleader over on the sideline trying to get my attention. I recognized her immediately. She had done some babysitting for us when the kids were little.

I walked over and asked what she wanted. "Mrs. Brence says that she needs to talk to you. She is right over there." I responded very quickly. "Go back over there and tell her that a game is getting ready to start out here, and I don't have time to talk to her."

Five minutes later I looked up and the same cheerleader is back on the sideline again. This time she obviously looked like she didn't want to be there. I walked over to see what was going on. She looked at me and said, "Coach, Mrs. Brence told me to tell you that you did have time to talk to her." I dropped my head and went over to see what she needed.

Don't underestimate the Subconscious Mind

"Success is a state of mind. If you want success, start thinking of yourself as a success."
--Dr. Joyce Brothers, psychologist

The older I get, the more I realize the power of the mind. In sports, the mental outlook is just as important as the physical condition. Most people don't think about how subconscious thoughts can affect you. If you take the time to examine and plan, you can do some things to control the subconscious mind. It can be a huge positive for your team if you do.

Planning takes pressure off everyone. Nobody likes negative surprises. Make sure you think things through so you don't have very many. For example, many teams have purposely designed cramped, dark visiting locker rooms for their stadiums. They want the opponent to deal with the negative when they arrive. Iowa University even went to the trouble of painting the visiting locker room pink. It sets a gentle, quiet tone. That's exactly the mood you want for your opponent before a game. Therefore, if you don't counsel your players about the Iowa dressing room before you get there, you risk a negative surprise that could be worth points on the scoreboard. Plan for every negative situation. Talk to your players about what to expect.

Create an environment where the highlight of the player's day is to be at practice. If you can create this environment, you have the odds in your favor. Great teams are usually happy teams. If the environment is positive, well planned and organized, then people will respond. They will fight for you. You don't have to make it easy. Just make it fun and positive.

Be careful what you say. Respect your opponent, but don't put them on a pedestal. Every team has flaws. Train your players to handle everyone the same. It will pay off in the long run. The best approach is to realize that on any given night you can beat anyone. At the same time, on any given night anyone can beat you.

With the proper people, talk about subconscious thoughts openly. We are getting into deep issues here. How do you know what everyone on the team is thinking? Get input from the correct people. Sometimes it might be a captain. Other times it might be the coaches. It might even come from a trainer or a manager. One thing is for sure, a smart head coach thinks about where his team is mentally. Try to spin issues your way. Talk openly about some awkward things if you think it will help. Just by mentioning something you can change someone's thought pattern.

Point the finger at yourself

Murphy's Law tells us that if it can go wrong then it probably will. No matter how smart you are it is inevitable that something will go wrong somewhere down the line. When something does go wrong many leaders tend to start blaming others. However, a smart leader will handle things another way.

List the positives. There are always positives in any situation. Make a list of all the things that worked well.

List the negatives. Look for reasons not excuses. List the problems, breakdowns and mistakes on paper. You will want to get feedback from your staff.

Point the finger at yourself. Take responsibility for your organization. Own your failures. Don't blame other people. It was your responsibility to be ready for problems before they happened.

Give people the benefit of the doubt. You may be angry and upset, but you better be careful in what you say. Keep your cool until you get all the facts and have time to think things through. Don't rip into anyone. Give them all the benefit of the doubt. The truth will come out in the wash.

Document what you need to keep it from happening again. Create a new policy and get it on paper. Make sure everyone involved knows what to do next time. If you need to buy new equipment, do it.

The most difficult problem I ever dealt with as an athletic director was dealing with lightning. On threatening weather days I was glued to The Weather Channel. I was always trying to predict where the trouble was up in the sky.

One night we had three games going on at one time. A huge storm came in on us. I took it for granted that everybody knew what to do. But guess what? A lot of people didn't know what to do. When I called a delay, everybody scattered. Even the referees decided to go home. I was furious, but I quickly realized that it was really my fault. I shouldn't have taken anything for granted. It was very embarrassing for me, but it was a learning experience. I thought about it all night long. I made notes, and I was ready to fix the problems the next day.

The biggest positive was that nobody got hurt. We were lucky. Also, we evacuated the stadium very quickly. However, we had poor intelligence about the weather, and we were not organized for a delay.

I created some new policies. I made sure we had the best equipment possible to find out about lightning. I made sure everyone knew that when we stopped play it meant to take cover. We instituted an automatic thirty minute delay. After the delay, we would regroup and decide if we would continue to play.

Two weeks later we had an even more intense storm roll through. This time we executed our plan perfectly. We were fortunate. The first storm was actually a blessing in disguise.

Create a Nightmare for Your Opponents

If you can figure out a way to dominate your competition it will make you a huge success. Of course, that is much easier said than done. But if you don't address it, you won't even have a chance to accomplish it. You won't just fall into it. You will have to earn it.

Figure out what you can do in competition that will lead to domination. Examine your strengths first. Brainstorm and think about the things you do best. With a little extra work you can prepare a scheme that is virtually unstoppable. You just have to make the commitment.

Understand that it will always be an ongoing struggle. Before you even find this nightmare for your opponents, you must understand that it is only a temporary thing. Eventually, you will have to either adjust or abandon the plan. Realize the competition will adjust. You have to be able to fix a problem before it arises.

Create your identity. When you find this advantage, it will define you and your program. Be ready to capitalize on the brand you develop. Be ahead of the game. Don't let the game sneak up on you.

Realize that it will develop naturally. In 2003, the Plano Senior High football team didn't win a game. We went 0-10. It was very humbling and embarrassing. One of the ways we came back was listening to great coaches. Our entire staff went to the LSU football clinic in Baton Rouge. Nick Saban was the head coach at the time. His speech was about finding a way to dominate and create a nightmare for the opponents. It energized our entire staff, and we had a new, bolder attitude. We came back to Plano determined to figure out ways to dominate other teams.

Our answers evolved on their own time schedule. Historically, Plano had been a two back, run oriented team. We had become predictable and old fashioned. However, we knew there were many great things in our old offense. We didn't want to give up on what we knew would work. We just wanted to branch out a little.

We decided to implement a spread offense. We kept it very simple and focused on plays we knew we could execute. Then we blended the old offense with the new offense to create a hybrid attack. All of a sudden, we had three offenses. We had our old stuff, our new stuff, and a mixture of the two. We kept things very simple, but we looked complicated. The new offensive approach turned out to be a monster for us against the competition.

The result was that we were able to keep the defenses guessing, because we were so versatile with our formations. It was simple to us, but it was tough on the opponent's defense. It created a nightmare for them. It all started with a new mindset acquired from a football clinic. It evolved into a vision, and then it became a reality.

Evaluate Your Evaluations

"If past history was all there was to the game, the richest
people would be librarians."
--Warren Buffett, investor

*Few people enjoy being evaluated. It goes against human
nature. However, evaluations shouldn't be viewed negatively.
Evaluations should be used for performance enhancement.*

Closely scrutinize the evaluation points you use. What exactly
are your evaluation statements? Are they really relevant to the job
at hand? Many employers use the same evaluation tool year after
year when their organization has changed dramatically in the same
period of time. Look closely at the wording you use. Simplify the
statements, and make sure they are relevant.

Be flexible in your system. Effective evaluation systems use
at least four main rankings. Exceeding Expectations, Meeting
Expectations, Below Expectations, and Unacceptable would
be examples. This is much better than just two rankings like
Acceptable or Unacceptable. Give your employees a little room.
A good idea is to include some type of documentation on any
ranking except Meeting Expectations. If someone has done
something outstanding, make sure you document it on his/her
evaluation.

Stress the evaluation system through the entire work cycle.
If you want a strong office staff you shouldn't wait until the
end of the year to start talking about evaluations. Start talking
about evaluations at the start of the year. Make your employees
understand what is expected of them. Show and tell them the
actual vehicle you will be using. You want a strong workforce that

can solve problems. Give them the **opportunity** to earn strong marks. One good idea is to have the supervisor carry around the evaluations with him. When something comes up whether good or bad, document it.

Don't fret over balancing the evaluation. If an employee is outstanding, tell him! One of the best ways to do that is to give him a strong evaluation. Just don't be a fake.

Cut your losses. Unfortunately, there reaches a point where you have to part ways with an employee. Take a backpedal step as often as you can to help anyone. However, when it reaches a point that you have to release an employee, make sure you have documentation to back your decision.

Create an environment where people are open to criticism. Young soldiers at West Point are taught early on to accept criticism. When people's lives are on the line there is no room for ego. If you can accept criticism and advice, you are way ahead of the game. Just because someone criticizes you doesn't guarantee that they are right and you are wrong. However, it will make you think things through.

Keep an eye on Team Synergy. With all this open criticism and intense evaluation going on, a strong leader has to be on his toes. Strong team spirit and energy leads to a powerhouse team. Morale is everything. Pay close attention to it.

CHAPTER 3
Coaching

51% players	49% coaches

The Community's Expectations

If you don't design your own plan, someone will design it for you."
--Jim Rohn, motivational speaker

If you decide to take on a high profile position in the community, you better understand the expectations. Expectations will vary from one township to another, but there will always be high standards. Before you leap, you better look.

Buy in to the whole, part, whole theory. One of the first things they should teach you when you go into education is to learn the whole, part, whole theory. It is really simple. Make sure when you start developing your program you look at the big picture. Vision separates leaders from followers. Always keep in mind the overall program and where you want it to go.

After you view the big picture, start breaking everything down into parts. All organizations will have different numbers when it comes to employees and resources. Break everything down into manageable parts.

After you break things into parts, go back and look at the big picture again. Make sure as the leader that you always schedule time for yourself to think and dream. That is how you can move forward to great things.

The program should be based on the leader. Don't delegate the future of your program to someone else. If you don't have the confidence to make decisions then you shouldn't be the leader.

Do things in threes. When I help my wife unload the groceries from the car, I grab three bags at a time. I know it may sound odd, but it works. Here are three objectives for a head coach.

1. **Do everything with integrity.** Integrity is number one, and nothing should ever even come close to challenging it. If you are working for the public, there are strong expectations about the influence you project on kids. You, as the leader, owe it to the community to make the most important thing the most important thing. Don't let your guard down, and don't waver in clutch times.

Eliminate the negatives. My wife and I had three boys. Football was very important to all of us. I knew the influence football had on my kids. I will tell you as a parent that the last thing I wanted was for my kids to learn to cuss and dip snuff from a coach. It is just not acceptable. Do not allow your coaches to use profanity. There is no place for it in the educational environment. It is against the law in Texas for tobacco products to be on a school campus. However, I know that doesn't stop a lot of coaches from using snuff and chewing tobacco. If you allow this on your team you are letting the community down. I always believed that what a coach did at his home was his business. However, what he does at school is a lot of people's business.

Name calling is another issue to avoid. Coaches should refer to the players by their names. Don't call a kid "Stupid" or "Bonehead." It is unprofessional and not necessary. I know people make mistakes, and I certainly don't want to create the thought that I was always perfect. I just want to express what I think is appropriate and what is not.

A few years ago the Indianapolis Colts and the Chicago Bears made it all the way to the Super Bowl. Both coaches, Tony Dungee of the Colts and Lovie Smith of the Bears, were African American. The media made a huge deal out of the fact that it was the first time two minority coaches made it to such a huge event as leaders. I greatly appreciated and respected that aspect of the game. However, another thing that set Tony Dungee and Lovie Smith apart was that neither used profanity or name calling around their players.

Establish clear and concise rules. Decide up front how you will handle issues like dress code, discipline, and school problems. The more you think ahead the better off you will be. Decide what discipline you will use for certain problems and stick to it. Don't wait until it happens. This kind of an approach will take a lot of pressure off of you as the coach. You can be disciplined and still have fun.

Coach the mindset. You have the policies in place. You are doing the right things. Now the most important thing is to coach these ideas into your team.

Create a curriculum on how you will go about teaching character and discipline to your team. You are the leader. You also need to be the head writer and planner. You are also the lead person when it comes to training your staff. There will be a **trickle down effect** from the head coach to the assistant coaches to the players to the community. **Reinforce your discipline** views all the time. You also need to **think about how you will handle Faith issues.** There are laws about the separation of church and state. As the leader you must know the law. If you know the laws and are comfortable with your interpretations it is easy to bring faith into your team. You just need to be aware that there are probably many different views on faith in the community. You are the coach not the preacher.

2. **Win.** You were not put into a high level position to lose. Winning is important. You just have to do it correctly, and it can be done.

Develop the correct work ethic. It all starts with the expectations of what the work ethic will be. How long will the hours be for the coaches? What will be the assignment configuration? How will the scouting report and game plan be put together?

I strongly believe that the head coach should set the work days and work hours far in advance of every phase of the season. Tell your coaches when they are supposed to come in for work and when they can go home. Remember, many of them are married and have kids. If you take their life away from them, how can it be the highlight of their day to be at practice? Set your work hours and stick to them.

One of the most important things you have to decide upon is your evaluation system. How will you evaluate players in practice? How will you evaluate game tape? How will you evaluate yourself, your scheme and your theories? Establishing a strong evaluation system is critical to your success.

Dictate your style. I am a big believer in playing to one's strengths. However, you have to figure out what your strengths are to do it. What offense, defense and special team style do you like? What is your pre-game ritual? Think of everything you possibly can and address it with your staff. It will become your reputation.

Style starts with theory. Your theory about how to win is everything. What do you feel in your heart will work for you and your team?

Focus on the players. You have a choice. You can keep the same style and scheme all the time or you can change due to your players' ability level. I think you should do both.

What's the plan? Organize your schedule and your staff so that you can put together the best game plan possible. There are a lot of ways to do it, but there are some basics that go into every single one.

Write out the itinerary. The plan starts with the itinerary. Write out what the practice schedule will be all week. How much will you condition? How much will you hit? When will you meet with the players? When does the bus leave? When will you get home after the game? When will you bring the kids in the day after the game? Think it all through, because it all matters. Get input from your staff, but don't delegate these decisions. These decisions will make you or break you. Post the itinerary on the board so everybody knows exactly what is going to happen and when. It takes a tremendous amount of pressure off of everybody. **The real trick to being a good head coach is figuring out just how hard to work the team.**

Execution is everything. After all this thinking and planning it comes down to one thing. How well do your players execute your plan? Stress to your players that your entire objective is to be where they are supposed to be when they are supposed to be there. After that, they have to make the play. Of course, a good coach can help them make the play, too. Make sure the players know what to do and when to do it. Get them in a position where they are confident, know the correct technique, and are in great physical condition. If you do all that, you have a great chance to win.

3. **Establish a great program.** Staying power is what you and your program will be remembered for as the years go by. It isn't good enough just to do it one year. You need to do it year after year. A lot of people can do it once, but can they do it over and over? The future should always be a part of your program.

Stay close to your feeder programs. Your middle school and sub-varsity coaches are a key to your success. I always thought there were two kinds of coaches. One type of coach wants to coach young players and doesn't really want to put in the long hours. The other type wants to be a varsity coach. You need both types. You want a balance, so you will have consistency at the middle school and sub-varsity level. You also need coaches who always want to move up to the varsity. The trick is to get a balance of both. If you have too many of the same type it will not be in the best interest of your program. Recognize this and it will be a great benefit to you. Get all your coaches involved and treat them with the respect they deserve. They are your lifeblood.

Be a camper. The one thing that I enjoyed the most about being the head coach at Plano was running summer football camps. I really worked hard at it. I did not delegate the camps to assistants. I was always there and ran the camps myself. Just about every kid who played on the junior varsity or the varsity while I was the head coach came through my summer camps. I focused on the basics. I taught them to tackle. I taught them to block. I taught them kicking game skills. The most important thing I taught them was the expectation side of things. Plus, we had a lot of fun. If you are the head coach you should feel obligated to the younger kids. They are the future. Get in there with them and develop them.

The head coach is the Chief Financial Officer of the program. You owe it to the community to make sure that your program has a strong financial base. It isn't the most important aspect of your program, but it is close. Gate receipts are important. You owe it to the community to do the best you can to pay your own way. You might not ever make it, but you can sure try. Manage your budget closely.

The head coach is in charge of the booster club. Booster clubs are what I called a "necessary evil." You probably need them in order to run your program the way you want. It is your choice. Just don't let them run you. Step up and take control.

Off-Season A to Z

"The two most powerful warriors are patience and time."
--Leo Tolstoy

If you really love to coach then the off-season is your favorite time of year. Off-season is the period of time that a coach really gets to teach the way he wants to teach. He has time for all the kids not just the ones who are playing in the games. He has time to teach, council, and mentor. He also has time to study, plan and develop his overall program. Strong leadership is essential to a good off-season. The head coach must be involved with everything. Every minute you waste will hurt you on the field in the fall.

Plan the big picture. Off-season starts before the season ends. The head coach should be planning, planning, and planning. There should be a big picture plan that carries all the way through to the start of two-a-days. You must create the correct environment. Remember, your objective is to create an atmosphere where the highlight of everybody's day is to be in off-season with you. If you do that, you should be very successful.

Break it down into 3 major areas. I was always a big believer that off-season broke down into three priorities. The first priority should be **character development.** High school coaches are more than just football guys. They owe the players, parents, school and community their best efforts to develop character skills in their players. If a high school coach doesn't realize this, he is very naïve.

The second priority should be **physical development.** Some programs have full time strength coaches, and some do not. It doesn't matter. All coaches should be involved in planning and executing the physical development of the players. I used to tell coaches all the time that they should study weight lifting, speed development, and flexibility as much as they studied the spread offense. Your job is to develop players. Off-season lasts from December to August. That's a long time. A well organized conditioning plan can make a huge difference.

The third priority is **fundamental skills**. I have never understood why more teams don't start coaching their players in fundamentals as soon as off-season starts. Granted, you can get carried away with fundamentals skills in off-season. However, it is about what the players know. When they know exactly what to do, you have a much better chance for success.

Stress character development. The head coach should develop a curriculum on character development. Use whatever materials you wish, but get a plan on paper. Think it all the way through. Be specific. Break the team down into parts so you can really get their attention. Developing strong character in kids is about consistency not volume. Produce short, concise, effective presentations for your players every day. That is much better than to preach to them for an hour once a month.

I heard a famous high school coach tell a great story at a clinic. He was a young assistant coach at the time. He was frustrated, because his team wasn't doing as well as he thought they should be doing. During the winter, his head coach challenged him to go to all the great programs in Texas and see them up close and personal. The coach went to Plano, Odessa Permian, Temple, and Highland Park.

When he returned, the head coach asked him what he learned. "Well, it wasn't that much different," he told the head coach. "But one thing I did learn is that our players are as good as theirs." The head coach quizzed him some more. "Then why do those guys win all the time?" The assistant coach thought a minute and responded. "The main thing was just the attitude. They just seemed like they were better people." The head coach realized very quickly how

125

he could elevate his program. "It's simple, then," he said. "Let's develop better people, and we will have better teams." That staff was at Converse Judson in the San Antonio area. Judson went on to become one of the great powerhouses in Texas High School football history.

Judson did it their way. They developed their own curriculum for character development. During the first two weeks of off-season they didn't even dress the players out in workout gear. They put them in a classroom environment and taught them character skills. They developed better people. Better people led to better teams.

Stress physical development. There are many different theories on training athletes. My advice is to study and train kids the best way you know. However, I do have some strong opinions on some issues. Weight lifting is crucial to development, but so are flexibility, quickness, speed and endurance. In football, you don't put a bench press out on the 50 yard line on Friday night and have a bench press contest. You play football. It's physical. It's nasty. It's competitive. You should have drills that challenge them to be good football players. At the same time, any drill that doesn't directly correspond to your sport is a waste of time. Develop drills that are sport specific and help your kids become better players.

Football involves running. If you don't run almost every day, I just don't know how you can condition your players to be faster. Some programs only run a couple days a week in off-season. I have never understood that.

Create an environment in your lifting and running that is as enjoyable to the kids as possible. If you kill them every day, how can they enjoy it? A coach walks a fine line on an issue like this. I really think the old "boot camp" mentality is not necessary. Kids in football want to work. They will do what you ask. You don't have to kill them. Teach them how to lift and run so they can do it properly on their own. Better yet, **they will want to do it on their own.** Kids are smart. They learn fast. Teach them how to lift so they are always working and developing. You can do that if you create the correct environment. Encourage your players to take the knowledge you give them and think for themselves.

Stress fundamental skills. There should be an evaluation process after the season for the coaches. They should look at the season from every angle. The staff might even decide to go in a new direction in their scheme. However, you can still find drills for your players that you know will help them.

I recommend starting with fundamental individual skills very early in off-season. Find a way to get the numbers down in groups so you can really teach the basics. Coach all the kids, too. Coach the best players and the worst players. Remember, consistency is better than volume. Ten minutes of individual a day is good. It gives the coaches more evaluation time. It is also fun for everyone.

Start moving into group work as off-season progresses. Be very detailed in what you want to accomplish so you don't waste time. Eventually, you can start working on all phases of your game. I always told our coaches, "Spring practice is not the time to teach the secondary how to adjust to formations. They have to know that by then. Spring practice is for the evaluation and improvement of our team." I always used that slogan to push the coaches to cover ground in off-season. The more information and coaching you give the players the better off you are. Remember, it isn't about what you know. It is about what the players know.

Make everything a game. I always loved spring practice. We had four weeks of full pads workouts usually starting in late April or early May. That is a long time. It takes skill to keep everybody interested. The more competitive you can make off-season, the better off you are. However, spring practice has got to be competitive or it will really drag.

Someone on our staff asked, "Why do we just play one spring game? Why don't we have a game every week?" We decided to have four spring games. We structured everything where the routine was just like it would be in the fall. This trained the young players to prepare for the grind. We would focus on getting them ready to play on Friday night. We tried to make the teams as competitive as possible. We kept the same routine as we used during football season. We had the scoreboard on for the fans. We used headphones. We tried to think of everything and get the players under the lights as much as we could. It made everything a lot more fun. Spring practice didn't seem to be drudgery, and the competition brought out the best in everyone.

Plan the summer. When school ends people start going their own way. A strong head coach will plan how he will handle summer issues. Everyone knows they must continue to work. However, there are so many variables it can drive you crazy.

If you set the base with your character development work, you will be ahead of the game. You must trust your players. They will travel. They will work. They have obligations. Teach them what to do and how to do it. Encourage them to work hard in the summer for themselves and the team. In Texas, we had 7 on 7 tournaments and summer off-season conditioning classes, but neither was mandatory. Some kids just couldn't participate. Don't worry about it so much. Do the best you can. It would be great if they were all there, but it probably won't happen that way. Trust them, and welcome them back in August.

It is the same for the coaches. Some will have summer jobs. Some will travel. They all have obligations. Develop a schedule for them if you choose, or just give them the summer off. It is up to the head coach. Whatever you do, create an environment in which the players and the coaches want to be in the field house working. If you don't, it will be counterproductive.

Center Practice around the Head Coach

A good leader can't get too far away from his followers."
--Franklin Roosevelt

When practice starts, everything should center on the head coach. Wherever he goes, that should be where the emphasis is centered.

Break practice into four areas. The four main parts of practice are offense, defense, special teams and conditioning. But here is the deal. The camera should follow the head coach. The intensity picks up every time he comes around. Focus the video on when the head guy is there.

Focus on your off-periods. When the head coach isn't around, the position coaches have an off-period or walk through drill. That is when they can slow down and really coach specifics. They are doing everything they can to get ready for the next period when the head coach and the head camera comes to them.

Conditioning is no different. When it is time to condition the head guy should be right in the middle of everything. It doesn't matter whether it is a running program or the weight room, he should be a part of it. I always liked everyone to run together. I thought it was good for team morale. If the coaches can participate in the running with the players, it is even more effective.

There are lots of advantages to this approach. The head coach can dictate the tempo of practice. He can evaluate the players up close and personal. Video of these periods can be the focus of the team in meetings. But the most important advantage of all is that it involves the head coach with the team on all important aspects of practice. It keeps the head coach in the middle of everything. That is where he should be.

Look Complicated but Be Simple

A little uncertainty is good for everyone."
--Henry Kissinger

Modern day offenses have their hands full trying to move the ball. To be successful, you have to be able to do it all and do it all well. The trick is to keep your offense versatile but simple for your players.

Think about the other side for a minute. Most defensive teams only get about 100 quality team practice repetitions during the week. Try to see things through their eyes. What can you do to control as many of those 100 reps as possible. Coaching defense is different than coaching offense. On offense, you control the play that is run. On defense, you have to react to everything. Use deception to your advantage during the week not just on game day.

Be versatile with everything you do. Be sure you can run, throw and use misdirection in every package. Make sure you can attack the middle of the field and both sidelines. Make sure you can throw deep, midrange and short from every formation. Do not make exceptions. You can do this and still be simple.

Develop your formations first. Make sure everyone on your offense understands the different formations you will use. Defensive football is about recognizing formations, adjusting to them then recognizing plays. After that it is about technique, effort, tackling and play making. It will be the formations that deceive the defense more than the actual plays. Think broad. Make the defense spend their time during practice adjusting to formations. It will take away from their time preparing to stop plays. If you make them think, you are slowing them down.

Develop a Power offense. I was always an option coach. That was my style of power football, but you need to use what you know and love. Choose the plays out of an under center quarterback offensive scheme that you want to run. Make sure you have a balanced attack, and make sure all your plays compliment each other. Don't get too complicated. Choose what you want to master. Don't try to do too much.

Develop an Open offense. The spread, shotgun offense can be ridiculously simple. Anyone that has ever run it can tell you that. Choosing what plays you want to use can get complicated. For example, I can show you three different ways to throw a quick pass. You, as the coach and leader, must decide what passes and runs you want to use each week. Make sure you are balanced. Make sure your plays compliment each other. Again, keep it simple, and start getting quality reps.

Develop a Hybrid offense. Now take the power offense and the open offense and mix and match the formations and plays. You will find that it is really easy to put the two offenses together. Now you have a third offensive attack, the hybrid.

Play to your strengths. If you can do all of this without changing personnel you can really get an advantage. Defensive coaches feed off personnel changes. You have to play to your strengths, but you can try to use deceptive personnel changes to fool the defense. But be careful with all that. Get your best players the ball. Don't outsmart yourself.

Answer all the questions. Make sure the chain of command is in place. Don't take anything for granted. Make sure these and other questions are answered.

1. Who will call the plays?
2. How will you get the play to the quarterback?

3. How will you handle personnel?
4. How will you handle the tempo of your offense?
5. What will you do when you are ahead?
6. What will you do when you are behind?
7. What will you do in short yardage and goal line situations?
8. What will you do in long yardage situations?
9. How will you run your two minute offense?
10. When will you use a trick play?
11. When will you gamble?
12. What will you run for a 2 point play?
13. What will you run in overtime?

Master the hurry up offense. You will give your team great confidence if they know they can come from behind with a hurry up offense. We always used sweat bands that had windows. We would put 5 or 6 plays on the sweatband. Every offensive player had one. All we had to do was call out a number, and we were off and running. We could keep any pace we wanted. We could even change the cards in the sweatbands if we wanted. The kids always knew we had the capability to rally quickly.

Put it all together and stress Execution. Simplicity and execution are the two keys. You can make it look complicated, but you need to make it simple for your players. Move the offense at different paces. You should have standard pace, fast pace, hurry up and slow pace. Whatever you do, just make sure you can execute the plays. If you can't execute a certain play, then don't run it in a game until you master it.

Time your Emotional Peaks

Most ballgames are lost, not won."
--Casey Stengel, baseball manager

*Gearing up for an emotional game or event takes some skill.
It is especially important to know what you are doing if you
are the leader of the group. There are many different ways to
approach a big game.*

Set the agenda. Start thinking about how you are going to gear
up yourself and your team way in advance. Think it through and
make a plan.

Stress to your team to wait for the game. Many a game has been
lost because a team peaks emotionally early in the week before
the game is played. The excitement is high, especially with young
people. It is human nature to get excited, but it must be tempered
so your fire won't burn out before the game.

Get your rest. The only way a human being can recharge his
battery is through sleep. Make sure your people are getting their
rest. Make a big deal out of it to everyone.

Pay close attention to how hard you are working your team.
The coach must know how hard to work his team. It is both a
talent and a skill to feel that fine line. Trust your instincts on how
you should handle it. Just make sure you are paying very close
attention to your players' body language.

Don't allow anything new into the game plan late in the week.
Do not over coach. It won't be about you. It will be about the
players. If you bog them down mentally, it will hold them back
emotionally and physically.

Bore them to sleep the night before the game. Some games just stay with a coach forever. The night before the 1993 state championship game, I made a huge mistake.

We were playing Converse Judson the next day at Baylor Stadium in Waco. We always watched film at 8:00 the night before every game. We were staying at a hotel in Waco. An assistant coach had told me about a highlight film he had made of our playoff run. We decided to show it at the end of the 8:00 meeting.

The meeting started and everyone was excited. I did nothing to tone things down. Then we showed the highlight video. It was awesome. Everyone was sky high and ready to play the game.

Everybody on our team, including me, was so excited about the highlight tape and the game that we couldn't sleep. The Texas 5A State Championship game in those days always started at high noon. Judson came out ready to go, and beat us. We did not play well.

After that, I always tried to bore the players to sleep the night before the game. The next year we went back to the state game and played Katy, Texas. This time I planned everything out before the trip. Everyone was asleep by 11:00 o'clock. We showed another highlight tape after the pre-game breakfast. We showed up alert and ready, and we won the state championship.

The Fullback Coach

What gets measured gets done."
--Peter Drucker

Sometimes the quickest way to success is to simplify. Figure out what the most important issue is in your organization, and assign it to the right person. Often he turns out to be a big difference maker.

Start new employees out with a specialized job. Nobody has a lot of time to wait for results. Therefore, it is a good idea to assign a new or especially young employee to one specific task. If he isn't overloaded, he will have a much better chance of being a difference maker. Keep it simple. Figure out where your organization needs to improve, and assign it to the new guy.

Think of the future. As time goes by, move the new guy to another specialized job. If he is an outstanding employee he will take on more and more responsibility. The main issue will be that you have an expert in a certain specialized field. It will take a lot of pressure off the boss to have that knowledge on the staff. Be careful about spreading your people too thin. You will end up with a lot of people who know a little about a lot. You won't have any expertise.

Expect immediate results. For years at Plano we had one coach who focused only on the middle linebacker position. Our defense was designed for the middle linebacker to make tons of plays, so it was a good setup.

The years went by, and I became the head coach. I kept the middle linebacker coach, but I also always thought we should do the same thing with the fullback position on offense. Fullback was a thankless position. He rarely got the ball, because he was mainly just another offensive lineman. However, without excellent fullback play we could never move the ball. I talked about a fullback coach often, but I never followed through with it.

Finally, when our backs were up against the wall because of losing and mediocre seasons, I followed my instincts. I assigned a young, first year coach the fullback position. It was a huge success. Our offense went from ordinary to outstanding. Our entire staff realized that the difference was the play of the fullback position. .

Don't overextend young employees. Give them simple assignments with direct instructions. You will be the one who ends up benefitting the most.

Don't Take Captains for Granted

He who would be a leader must be a bridge."
--Unknown

Who you choose to be on your subordinate leadership team is critical to your success. Athletic teams are just like business organizations. Most upper level leaders simply choose people they feel will do the best job. But stop and think about it. Doesn't it make sense to have a built in system to define who will be qualified to be a captain?

Define exactly what you are looking for in a captain. Meet with your coaches and write down what you want in your leadership team. Make it very clear, and put it on paper. It will become a staple of your program for years to come.

Make them apply. Announce to your team that you are accepting applications to become team captain. Make out the form yourself. Ask the questions that need to be asked. You will find out who is interested in really executing the job. Don't leave underclassmen out of the process. You will find out who your younger leaders are, and it will give them a chance to study the process.

Make the selection process very clear. There are many ways to choose the leader. You can have team elections. You can assign captains. You can let the coaches choose. It is important how you choose the leader, but it is more important that everyone associated with the team knows exactly how it will be done.

Hold them accountable. Weak leaders will kill your program. Bad examples are just as influential as good examples. Don't decide who the captains are and then forget about them. Meet with your leaders regularly and have an organized plan about what you demand from your leadership.

Realize the importance of the captain level leadership on your team. It's simple. This one issue could very well be the difference between success and failure.

Hidden Yardage

"How you gather, manage and use information will determine whether you win or lose."
--Bill Gates

You sure can't talk about football without talking about special teams. After all, they do call it football. It shouldn't amaze anyone that what happens when the ball is kicked still usually decides a close game.

Don't go overboard. Some coaches go overboard coaching kicking. Some coaches don't coach it enough. The kicking game makes up approximately 20% of a game. Therefore, devote 20% of your practice time to it. The key is personnel. Every head coach wrestles with a common issue dealing with kickoffs, punts and field goals. Do you play your starters, or do you play your backups? I say do both. Try your hardest to play as many kids as possible that do not start on offense or defense. Football is a numbers game. You want kids to come out for your program and have fun. If you don't let them play, how can you promote your numbers? However, if they can't get the job done, you have to replace them. You owe it to your players to play as many kids as possible. There is one exception. Whoever handles the ball better be one of your best players, period.

Keep your scheme simple and easy to execute. NFL coaches used to say that Vince Lombardi's Green Bay Packer teams were easy to scout. They were just difficult to stop. You are better off to keep it simple and execute, especially in the kicking game.

Devote one entire practice to the kicking game. Take one practice early in the season and devote it solely to the kicking game. Don't even try to do anything else. Go through every kicking game situation you can imagine. It is long, tedious and boring. It is also necessary. I always had the theory that I didn't want my players worrying about any kicking game issue the day before a game. By then, you better have everything down pat. There is enough pressure on them as the game gets close. Don't bog them down with a lot of coaching, especially in the kicking game as the game gets close. It will affect the entire mood of the team.

The Winning Edge. Talk up the importance of the kicking game. We used to call it "The Winning Edge." We really believed every kicking play gave us an opportunity to win the game. Everybody in football knows how important the kicking game is on the scoreboard. The problem is that the kicking game isn't glamorous; so make it glamorous!

Count the hidden yardage. Our staff came up with this system years ago. We used 30 yards on any kicking play as our gauge. For example, if we punted to our opponent 45 yards and there was no return, we counted that as +15 yards. If we punted the ball 45 yards and the opponent ran it back 30 yards, we counted that as -15 yards. We went through every kicking play that way. It will reveal hidden yardage. Our goal was to gain 100 yards in hidden yardage per game.

Put somebody in charge. Some head coaches just don't have time to be the offensive or defensive coordinator because of their duties at the school. Instead, they become the special team's coordinator. That is a great idea. However, if the head coach isn't coordinator for special teams, somebody else needs to be the coordinator. There is too much coaching to be done not to have someone in charge.

Keep a Few Tricks in Your Bag

"There are more upsets in bowl games, because the underdogs have a month to read about how they are going to get beat."
--Bud Wilkinson, football coach

Everybody loves a good trick play. However, they can be dangerous. If you are a coach of any sport you need to have at least one trick up your sleeve. You just need to know the risk and reward. More importantly, you need to have a plan.

Study the scheme. Don't just go for some idea an assistant coach throws out there. Study everything about the play against all defenses. Get the answers to all the tough questions. Does it make sense? Will work on paper? What could go wrong? Can we execute it?

Be original. Oldies are goodies, but people have already seen them. Come up with your own trick play. Be creative. Match the play to the situation. Put your name on it.

Create a bank of tricks. Before the season starts have all your tricks ready in a package. Have one for every game if possible.

Sell it to the players. Become the best salesman since Lee Iacocca. Sell your players on why these plays will work. Give them fun names. Make it a game inside the game. The players will love it.

Work all your trick plays into the practice schedule. Every day work one or two trick plays into the master schedule, so you are getting quality reps every practice. After a few days you have quite an arsenal. But you must get a lot of repetition. Never run a trick play in a game until you have it down pat.

Look for the opportunity. Study days before the game which trick play you will run and when you will run it. Make sure all your coaches and players know the information. The odds are much better if everybody is in on the action.

Have a way out. Always have a way to check out of a trick play. Train your players to recognize disaster and call off the deception. It will give everyone on the team confidence in what you are doing.

Be prepared for the worst and hope for the best. That is all you can do when you gamble, and trick plays are gambles. Train everyone involved about the risk and reward. Prepare them for success or failure. If the trick play works, you might follow it with a no huddle play.

Give everyone on the team ownership. You must realize that it is much deeper than just a trick play. It is a vehicle for positive team morale.

Practice the Ugly

Opportunity is missed by most people, because it is dressed in overalls and looks like work."
--Thomas Edison

If you want to win, you better take the time to practice every conceivable situation your team will deal with in a game. The deeper you go in the playoffs, the harder it is to win. A great coach will be ready no matter what the situation. Preparing for several different situations takes a lot of planning, sweat and patience, but it can be done.

Keep a log of specific situations. Coaches watch other games. A good coach feels situations and watches what other coaches do in those situations. Always carry a notebook to document what you see. Remember, your memory will fail you. Write everything you think is important on paper and keep it.

Write out your plan. Devise specific plays for every situation during the off-season. Keep it in a book. Script it into your practice schedule when you start the season. Make sure you educate your team on what to do. Don't underestimate how easy it is to draw a pass interference penalty on the opponent. If you think it through, you can tilt the odds in your favor. Practice 50 yard field goals. Even if you aren't good at it, the players will know at least you have a shot in that situation. It is like everything else. If you keep talking about it and practicing it, someday you will be good at it.

Hold your patience and your resolve to practice the ugly.
Coaching specific situations is tedious, hard work. It's ugly. Often you are out in hot, humid weather. It's easy to give up on coaching these situations. Here is how to make the most out of your time.

1. Go over it several times with your coaches and players in the classroom. Work on it mentally first. Be very detailed in your approach.
2. Set the stage in practice. Make sure everyone knows the situation.
3. Use the Whole, Part, Whole theory. Go through the whole play, and then break it down into parts. Run the whole play again. Get quality reps.
4. Talk about when you will use your ammo. Demand that your players be attentive and know what is going on in these situations. Great teams have smart players.

Dream. After you get a plan in place, start dreaming about using it. Remember, the difference between leaders and followers is innovation. Dream about how you will win a game in an unbelievable comeback situation.

How about a "Yes, Sir?"

To be well liked, you have to be the one to reach out first."
--Dale Carnegie

*Teaching kids discipline is like anything else. You have to get
repetition. Parents have to be strong enough to correct poor
behavior on the spot. It is uncomfortable and embarrassing.
However, the longer a parent waits to correct his child, the
easier it is to let issues slide. My mother in law told me once
that she told her kids she wanted everyone to like them. That
was why she disciplined them.*

Everyone needs to be on the same page. Parents have to be
together on discipline, but they also better be ready for differences
of opinion, too. The key is to establish correct behavior and
discipline around others at an early age.

Show people how to do it. When I was coaching we had a stern
rule. The players answered the coaches with a "Yes, Sir" or "No,
Sir." The coaches were trained to greet the players the same way.
I have said "Yes, Sir" or "No, Sir" to kids many a time. It is a
great example to young people. Handling it this way makes it
habit forming for everyone in the program.
  When a player didn't respond properly I would just ask. "How
about a Yes, Sir?" I wasn't mean spirited. I just asked them for
some courtesy. I don't ever remember not getting the response
I wanted. It was a little thing, but it reinforced the kids to be
respectful.

Go the extra mile. Respect for everyone by everyone also leads
to friendship. Take it a step further and ask a few questions. Teach
the kids how to interact with adults.
  We had a player once named Jordan. His mother taught English

with me at Plano Senior High. Jordan was a little guy who didn't get to play much, but he took great pride in being a Plano football player.

One day his mom caught me in the hall and told me that she had a tough problem. It turned out that Jordan was an accomplished musician. He had been asked to play in a big concert in San Francisco. However, he would have to miss a football game on Friday night, so he wouldn't go to the concert. I told his mom I would take care of it.

I saw Jordan in the hall the next day. "Jordan," I said. "you realize that you will go a lot further with your music than you will with football. You need to go to this concert."

Jordan said okay, and we kept talking. Finally I said, "By the way, what do you play?" Immediately, I saw a hurt look on his face. "Coach," he said, "don't you know I play weak corner?"

Corporal Punishment

"Speak properly, and in as few words as you can, but always plainly; for the end of speech is not ostentation, but to be understood." --William Penn, statesman

These days I wouldn't recommend that anyone use corporal punishment in any professional setting. However, many young parents still feel it is appropriate in their homes. I don't think there are any experts on this subject, but there are many of us who have experience.

Keep your cool. The biggest problem with corporal punishment is anger on both sides of the issue. Somebody did something that warranted a spanking. Many times the discipliner is a lot more dangerous than the disciplinee. Never give a swat to your child when you are really angry. It will be counter productive and could turn into a disaster. Think it out, cool down and serve out the punishment when you are calmer.

One swat is enough. I never bought into the theory of swatting a kid several times. How do you know when to stop? When you are disciplining a child, one swat is enough. Make it firm. I always felt your bare hand was enough, but I understand that moms might want to use a board on ornery boys.

Just remember this. If you are going to use corporal punishment, make it work. Don't be a wimp. Spank them hard on the tail. Never abuse them. You have to get their attention, or you are wasting your time. If you don't make it a deterrent, it will make the situation worse. As boys grow older and get bigger, they might challenge you. If you don't show authority, they will laugh at you. I always thought it was good that the kids were a little scared of somebody.

Be sure you understand the big picture. We stopped using corporal punishment in the Plano schools years ago. However, at one time we used it almost every day. We had a coach once who had a troublesome kid in his Physical Education class. The kid was always causing problems and being disrespectful. The coach finally had enough. He brought him into the coach's office and gave him a lick. After that, the coach didn't have any trouble with the kid. They actually became pretty good friends. One day the kid was a no show. Everybody wondered where he went. A couple of weeks later we found out the troublemaker kid was actually an undercover narcotics agent.

Beware of the Man Child

Some kids are physically way ahead of other kids. Whenever you see a young kid with an adult's body you should be aware. It's not always such a good thing.

Think of the pressure on the kid. There is such an emphasis on athletics in our country we often get things out of whack. Face it; there are some kids who grow and advance physically much faster than other kids. On the surface, people may think this is a great deal. However, look closer and you will see some real problems. You have to realize that the chronological age and the body sometimes don't match up right. You still have a twelve year old kid. He just has the body of an eighteen year old. It can put a lot of pressure on a kid, especially in athletics. People will have these unreal expectations for the student-athlete, but he probably just wants to be like all the rest of the kids.

Things can come too easy. On almost every team there is always the kid who can sit around and never work, but he is still a better athlete than anyone else on the team. You better watch this kid closely. It is easy for him to develop terrible work habits, because sports are just too easy. The next problem is a total lack of discipline. Also, people tend to enable these kinds of kids. Poor work habits can creep into their school work. A veteran coach usually has seen this situation many times.

The other kids usually catch up. Nature has a funny way of catching up to you. When I was coaching, I saw it all the time. One of three things usually happened. The first instance was that all the rest of the kids caught up or even moved ahead. Counsel this kid and make sure he has a strong work ethic. It can be devastating when all of a sudden, he isn't even good enough to play.

Another instance is when the kid has developed such poor work habits that he can't compete socially with the other players. He has been passed on in school, because he was such a great athlete. Everybody covered for him all those years when he got in trouble. He developed a terrible work ethic. Arrogance can be developed that becomes deep seeded into the personality. The other kids who are used to working go right by him.

The third instance is the kid who keeps his humility all the way through and handles the situation correctly. If he has the proper guidance from home and from school, he might make it to the big time some day. As a coach, just remember to tell the kids this one fact. Athletics ends eventually for everyone. That includes the Hall of Famers, too. It came to an end for Troy Aikman and Emmitt Smith just like it came to an end for an average high school player. The timetable was just different.

What can we do for these kids? The first thing we can do is to recognize these kids. It's like everything else. It's all about communication. Talk to them about it. Don't pamper them, and don't show them favoritism. Make sure they understand they are blessed with a great body. Also, make sure they know how things may go in the future. Many people believe that if you don't establish discipline in a kid by age 8 or 10 you never will establish it. Make sure the "Man Child" tag doesn't become a curse.

Wild Indians

"Victory without honor is like an unseasoned dish. It will satisfy your hunger, but it won't taste good."
---Joe Paterno, football coach

Make sure you communicate to your players how important it is to learn to keep their mouths shut. High level sports are too competitive to hand over any advantage. Why would anyone want to give the opponent an emotional charge before a game?

We had an offensive lineman once who was out for the season with an injury. This lineman was a great player who went on to play Division 1 football. He was always saying the wrong thing at the wrong time. He was so big that he thought no one could challenge him. He called himself Big Boy.

We went on the road to play a team that was in the middle of a 15 game losing streak. They were the weakest team we would play all year. It was natural for our players to be overconfident. Our team came out of the locker room, walked the field and went back into the locker room before the game. Big Boy wasn't playing this night, so he decided to stay outside and watch the other team walk the field. He commenced to tell them how bad they were and how we were going to humiliate them. I'm sure he was about as arrogant as he could be as he said it, too. Soon the game started. Nobody on our side knew anything about what Big Boy told the other team.

Of course, we barely escaped with a win. It turned out to be the most physical game we played all season. The team that was supposed to be so weak turned out to play the hardest, toughest football we saw all year. They played with a tremendous fire.

After the game, I met the other coach at midfield. "Tell ole Big Boy over there, thanks," he said. "That was the best our guys have played all year."

My Worst Day as a Coach

"Follow you instincts. That is where true wisdom manifests itself."
--Oprah Winfrey

Most coaches might have trouble figuring out the worst day they ever had in coaching. However, for me it was easy. The day and the story revolved around my oldest son, Ryan. The story is interesting even though it was pathetic on my part. But the lesson it taught me was invaluable.

Ryan was a sophomore in high school at the time. Plano has a unique school system. The 9th and 10th graders are at a different campus than the 11th and 12th graders. It was a big deal to move a kid up from the 10th grade to the varsity, but we could do it. During Ryan's sophomore year, we were really struggling at the senior high. We needed some more defensive backs which was Ryan's position. In the third game of the season we gave up almost 50 points in a loss to Duncanville. Our secondary missed a ton of tackles. During the weekend, the conversation quickly turned to our younger players who could help us in the secondary. Ryan's name came up immediately.

I had a bad feeling about the whole thing. Ryan was a very good player at the time, but I just didn't feel he was quite ready for the varsity. The coaches tried to convince me otherwise. I heard about it all weekend. They needed him up on the varsity. I always fretted about bringing up any underclassman, but this particular case was my own son. Finally, I gave into pressure, and we decided to move him on up on Monday.

Over the weekend my mother, Pearl, got wind of what was going on in Plano. I'm sure one of my two other kids, Beau or Collin, told her on the phone. Pearl never interfered with either our football or child rearing. However, she had seen the vicious play in 5A football up close and personal. On Monday morning, she called me up. She never called me during the day like that. "I heard you were moving Ryan up to the varsity," she said. "Don't do it. He is too young. He will get hurt." I will never forget the tone of her voice. I explained that the decision had been made and that he was moving up today.

That is only the beginning of the story. I decided as the head coach that we had to put in some new tackling drills. I didn't think we could tackle anybody, so we needed the work. We organized these tough, hard hitting drills for our defense. They were to begin right at the start of practice.

You have to understand that if you were an underclassman like Ryan, you had to ride a bus over to the senior high. He was one of the last kids dressed and out on the field. So what does he do? He jumps right into the drill and goes against a 220 pound linebacker right off the bat. I was busy moving around and missed what happened next.

On the very first tackling drill Ryan participated in, he dislocated his shoulder completely out of socket. He got up and got back in line. He went again. This time he ducked his head and looked like the biggest wimp that ever played football. Of course, his shoulder was demolished. What did I do? I jumped all over him. I tell him to get back in line and show some courage as a football player. He gets back in line and goes again. Finally, I realize he is hurt. The trainer tried to put his shoulder back in place, but he couldn't do it. Ryan ended up at the hospital for hours waiting for a doctor who could put it back into place.

Practice got even worse. About 20 minutes after we got Ryan out of there another player suffered a compound leg fracture while trying to make a cut. It scared the rest of the kids to death. It took over an hour for the paramedics to get him secured and off to the hospital. I was walking on eggshells the rest of practice.

I will never forget how I felt that day. I still haven't recovered from it. What compounded the whole thing was that I went against my basic core belief. If I believe anything, I believe that you should trust your instincts. I didn't listen to my instincts, and my son got hurt. And not only that, I didn't mind my mother.

Be Strong with Your Hands

One thing that anyone can do to make himself a better athlete is to work on the strength of his hands. It is as much mental as it is physical. Face it; most of the great athletes have great hands. For many, natural talent with the hands does not come easy. You have to work at it.

Be strong with your hands was said on our practice field a thousand times. You can't be timid with your hands. Be aggressive. Reach out there and grab the ball with authority. Deliver the blow with tremendous hand force. Emphasize strength and attitude. It applies to offense, defense or special teams. Always remember, strike them before they strike you.

Develop Hand-Eye drills. There are a hundred different drills you can use for your hands. Some sports don't require great hands but most do. If you can keep your eye on the ball it will help you in every technique.

Close games usually come down to one thing. One team will make a big play to win. How do they do it? Somebody makes a play with his hands. You can define athletic ability in a lot of ways, but hand skills have got to be a factor.

Deal with Booster Clubs Effectively

"Why would a coach want to create his own lynch mob? "
--Bum Phillips, football coach

In today's athletic world, booster clubs are not a requirement, but often they are a necessity. High school and college athletic programs are stretched financially as far as they can go. But beware of the booster club. There are a ton of stories out there about booster clubs gone wrong. Managed correctly, they can be an asset that can translate into points on the scoreboard. Just make sure you keep things in order.

Make sure everyone knows who is in charge. As a head coach, I wouldn't be associated with any booster club that I couldn't control. This very issue is where most clubs go wrong. The coach must control the booster club, period. If he doesn't, expect chaos to ensue.

Keep it simple. There will be rules and regulations required from the college, school district and even the state. You must follow the guidelines. After that, keep things simple. Don't create complicated bylaws, elections, etc. Set your bylaws in place, and stick to them.

The coach should choose the leadership. I have never agreed with any booster club that has an election for chief leadership. Choose a club leader that agrees with you in your general perception of the program. State your view on this issue up front.
  Most clubs use parents for the top leadership role. Be careful here. Obviously, it is in your team's best interest to appoint a level headed person. It also is important that you address his child

in this matter. It is best if he is a top level player. People won't question playing time so quickly if he is a top player. That might not be politically correct, but it is important. Think about the pressure on the student-athlete. He didn't ask that his mom or dad be the booster club president. All of a sudden there is a new kind of pressure on everyone in the household. As the coach, make it perfectly clear that he will be treated like everyone else. Address the ups and downs of the whole situation. Warn the parents and the student about what could come up during the season.

I always picked a vice-president out of the junior class. His main job was to observe everything that happened in the club for a year. I also put the vice-president in charge of the checkbook. He paid all the bills and was in charge of overseeing the budget. That way, when he became the president, he should know the money trail all the way through the year. Those were his two main responsibilities. You will have to choose other people to help. Make sure you define their jobs in detail.

Keep everyone together on fund raising and budgeting issues. A booster club is like any other business. It must be organized and efficient. Decide where you want to spend the club's money. Also, what types of fund raisers will you use for money? Go slow, and be careful. Make sure that you don't have someone in the club taking off on their own and getting away from the group. Strong leadership is critical for success.

Plan your meetings. The head coach and the booster club president should put together an agenda for all meetings. The coach should always be at the meetings. If he misses meetings he will lose control, and he is asking for trouble. It is all about communication.

Keep everything above board. If you have read through this book so far you understand that this is a recurring theme. Don't make off the cuff comments. Never use profanity. Be a consummate professional in your dealings with the club. Don't take anything for granted. Remember the key to the whole thing; the head coach must be in control of the club, and he must communicate with everyone involved.

How to Tackle

"You don't have to be the biggest to beat the biggest."
--Ross Perot

I always took a lot of pride in teaching young football players how to tackle properly. I just couldn't resist writing about my views on this subject. It doesn't matter if it is the NFL or the little leagues, proper tackling technique is the same at any level.

Keep your head up. Never drop your head in football. Almost all head and neck injuries are because of a player dropping his forehead down and leading with the top of his head. It is the coach's duty to enforce this with every player. Never allow a player to drop his head in any situation without addressing it immediately.

Lead with the V of the neck. The V of the neck is the line from the head to the tip of the shoulder. It forms a V. Proper tackling starts here. If the football player leads with the V of the neck and keeps his head up, his chances of injury are very slim. This will also give his natural body momentum a chance to help him.

Aim at the legs. Keep your head up, lead with the V of the neck and aim right around the knees. This is the safest way to tackle for both the defender and the ball carrier. During the course of the game you will get your chance for the big hits. Take them when you feel the time is right, but the rest of the time tackle like a pro.

Club your arms around the legs. Keep your head up, lead with the V of the neck, aim right at the knee level, and then club your arms around the knees. This will bring down any back.

Drive your legs through the tackle. Keep your head up, lead with the V of the neck, aim at the knee area, club your arms around the knees, and then drive your legs through the tackle. You can tell that I love repetition.

Use the best tackling drill. The best tackling drill I ever used was one we developed in football camp with kids. Line the players up in lines with a light standup dummy in front of every kid in the front of the line. Have the player in the front of the line get on his back. When the coach blows the whistle, the players get up off the ground and go through the process we have learned. Keep your head up, lead with the V of the neck, aim at the knee level, club up with your arms, and drive your legs through the tackle.

Many coaches think you need to get out on the field and have blood and guts types of drills. They usually don't teach proper tackling, and they discourage a lot of kids from playing football.

Act like you have made a tackle before. Taunting is for amateurs. Everyone will be watching, so act like you have done it a hundred times. Because if you tackle like this page tells you to, you will.

The Toughest Job in Sports

"Real courage is when you know you are in trouble before you begin, but you begin anyway and see it through no matter what."
--Harper Lee, author

Have you ever been on a bad athletic team? You haven't seen the entire experience of sports if you haven't been in that situation. It is a very difficult position especially when the realization hits that you have a very long season ahead of you. What do you do when you are getting killed on the field? How do you handle it? Here are some ways to cope.

Check your ego at the door. The first thing you have to do is humble yourself. You have to understand that "it is what it is." Don't make excuses, and don't belittle your players. Keep everything above board, and never compromise your ethics. As the leader you have to be above the situation.

Become the biggest cheerleader on the team. No matter how bad the score gets you need to cheer and be positive. Look for the smallest glimpse of success and progress. Be loud, and be positive. Everyone on the team will feed off the leader. If he is upbeat, positive and very enthusiastic it will set the mood no matter what the score. Sometimes you have to force the issue and act.

Break it all down. Put more quality time into your team. My mentor, Tommy Kimbrough, used to hold his thumb and forefinger just a tiny space apart and say, "Just try a little bit harder." Study every aspect of your team and figure out how to improve.

Stay in control of the environment and atmosphere. You can somewhat control the environment. You might not have a great team now, but you can create one for the future. The trick is to make everyone love to come to practice every day to be with you.

Throw it Through the Inside Arm

At times when I was coaching at Plano, I was known as the most conservative coach in the state. I just came up in a generation of conservative, option football. That was what I knew and what I did. I moved up to the varsity staff in 1983 as the wide receiver coach. I had never played the position in my life. We rarely threw the ball, but I knew that when we did pass, we had to make it work. Most of the time, however, we viewed the wide receivers as extended offensive linemen. We had simple assignments. We had to get the play from the coach to the quarterback. We had to make sure we got lined up straight. We had to block defensive backs, and we had to be ready to catch a pass when an opportunity came. But we did study the passing game, and we used it well. One of my favorite accomplishments was that we finally did transition our offense to a more balanced attack before I retired. It took years to do it. I feel strongly about how to coach passing.

Throw it through the inside arm. I know in college and the pros they target all kinds of points on the body, but high school isn't the pros. I challenge you to look closely at why high school teams miss passes. Most of the time, they don't throw to the correct shoulder. If you teach your quarterbacks to hit the proper spot, you can throw the ball on anybody.

Don't waste time in practice. We used 4 quarterbacks at a time. Two would start the drill and two would wait until the next repetition. We had two lines of receivers. We always started together using centers. Our warm-up throws were our shortest routes in the game plan. Each quarterback threw 3 times. Then we switched sides, so all the quarterbacks got 6 reps on every route. Next, we moved to the second shortest route. We went all the way to the end of our passing tree.

We focused totally on fundamentals of both the quarterback and the receivers. We used two coaches when we could, but one guy could run this drill. We emphasized that the quarterback take the snap, use perfect footwork, and then hit the receiver exactly where we wanted him to throw. We always made a big deal to the quarterback to immediately realize where he was after he threw the ball. If his footwork was good, he would be right where he was supposed to be. We also focused on touch on the ball. "Firm, with touch," was our slogan to the quarterback.

The receivers worked on stance, get-off, route running, timing and catching the ball. After he caught the ball, we made a big deal about sprinting 20 yards downfield past a cone. It emphasized YAC (yardage after catch). A lot of coaches scream at kids when they don't catch the ball with their hands. Tell that to a receiver after a linebacker runs through his chest in a game. There is a time to absorb the ball into your pads. It is a great way to pull a kid out of a slump. I never used one handed ball drills. I was fundamentally opposed to it. Why reinforce a negative habit. If a kid goes for a ball with one hand in a game and misses the ball everybody in the stadium will be down on him. That said, there are times when a receiver has to go for a one handed catch. I always told them to catch it anyway they could.

Don't hold the ball. I never wanted the quarterback to hold the ball. Everything we did was on timing. I always instructed the quarterback to go through the process. He would take the snap, go through his proper footwork, find his receiver, go to the alternate receiver if necessary, and then take off running if nobody was open. I guess it comes from my option background, but I just don't like offenses where the quarterback just stands around in the pocket.

There was a secret. The last year I coached, I moved a young coach to the varsity staff. He had played quarterback his entire life, and he really wasn't ready to coach anything else. I said,

"Okay, you are the quarterback coach, and I will be the wide receiver coach. We will work together." The ironic thing was that I came in as the wide receiver coach, and I went out as the wide receiver coach. But I knew a secret. If the head coach is coaching the wide receivers, you know your team is going to pass.

Wild Indians 2

"A hunch is creativity trying to tell you something."
--Frank Capra, film director

Sometimes the best advice comes from the strangest places.
The leader should listen to everyone. You never know where
you will get good advice.

Watch and listen. A really strong leader will have eyes in the
back of his head. Without ever letting anyone see you sweat,
observe everything. It helps to write it down. What did you see?
What did he say? Don't overreact to anything. Just gather as
much information as possible, and start working on your decision.

Pay attention to common sense. In 1992, my first year as the
head coach at Plano, we got off to a tremendous start. We were as
good as anyone in the state. Then, boom, our starting quarterback
went down with a shoulder injury.

Back in the spring, I moved the best athlete on the team, a guy
named Mike Nelson, to backup quarterback. Mike had never
played quarterback. I just thought I was such a good coach that
I could mold him into what I wanted. Mike was already starting
at free safety, but now he would have to become the starting
quarterback. Needless to say, he wasn't ready. He dropped snaps,
fumbled pitches and made poor decisions. He also made some
great plays. The talent was there, he just needed better coaching
from me. In our last game of the season, we played a playoff game
at Texas Stadium. It was raining. Mike had trouble holding onto
the ball, and the Plano fans were really frustrated with him. We
lost the game.

All summer long all I heard was, "Whatever you do, don't put
Nelson back in at quarterback." You must realize that Mike Nelson
was a Division 1 player with a tremendous IQ. He was an honor

student and a great athlete. He also had great pride. He went on to play on the great Northwestern teams in the 90's under Gary Barnett.

Mike's senior season started. He was doing a great job as a free safety which was his natural position. We were winning games, but they were all low scoring affairs. A typical game for us would be to win 14-7. Mike was again the second team quarterback.

The Plano East game came along. They were great on defense, and we couldn't move the ball. Late in the game, Plano East scored to tie the game. All of a sudden over my left shoulder, I heard a chant from the student body. "We want Nelson. We want Nelson." At first, it really made me mad, but then I realized that the students were right. I was tired of beating my head against a wall trying to move the ball.

Mike returned the kickoff and came over to the sideline. "Hey," I said to Mike, "catch your breath and get some water. I am putting you in at quarterback." Nelson was exhausted, but I could see the flame in his eyes when I gave him the news.

We get nothing on the first two plays. On third and ten Mike comes up from the bench and grabs my shoulder. "I'm ready to go, Coach," he says. I look at him and say, "All right, right pro 29 tight end load. That's our best play."

Nelson takes the ball and heads right. He makes one of the best runs in Plano football history scoring on a 70 yard touchdown run. We rolled through the rest of the season after that. Nelson led the way playing quarterback. We lost in the state championship game.

If you are in a high pressure situation, you need results. Try to understand the situation the best you can, and listen to everyone.

Production vs. Potential

"Give me a stock clerk with a goal, and I'll give you a man who can make history. Give me a man with no goals, and I'll give you a stock clerk."
--J.C. Penney, retailer

Sometimes looks can be deceiving. A good coach knows to be careful about getting carried away with a player's potential. Always keep in mind that the coach should have a solid evaluation system in place for all players. The cream should rise to the top. Time will tell who the best players are. Don't make decisions just based on the appearance of an athlete. Take production over potential.

Document the data. During off-season and pre-season document all kinds of information about your players. Keep records on strength, speed and agility. Pick the vehicle that you want to measure and stick to it. Give the players two or three opportunities to master the vehicles. Pick specific skills and subjectively evaluate the players. You can rate them 1 as poor and up to 5 as superior. Pick out 5 specific skills to measure the players and evaluate them. It will give you a place to start pre-season line-ups for your team.

Use video. I always believed that if you were not using video for practice and game evaluation, you were not doing everything you could to win. Coaching is not the business to just go through the motions. You have to go the extra mile to wade through all the videotape. Your memory will lie to you. You owe it to the players and the team to evaluate video on a regular basis.

Evaluate who can really do the job best. Coaches need to beware of the player who looks great but cannot produce on the field. The old "Looks like Tarzan, plays like Jane" theory happens more than you think.

Realize you can make a mistake. Many times the coach just doesn't have the time to evaluate as much as he wants. If that happens, mistakes can be made. When I first started out as a coach, baseball was my second sport. I would have over 100 kids try out for the team, and I only had a week to evaluate them. I made the first cut. The next day a couple of players came to me and said, "Coach, we don't want to tell you what to do, but you might have missed on Matt." They weren't disrespectful or anything. They just knew a little more information than I did about their friend. "Okay," I said, "let's get him back in here for another look." A few years later Matt was playing in the Philadelphia Phillies organization.

The Make Sure List

"In preparing for battle, I've always found that plans are useless, but planning is indespensible."
--Dwight Eisenhower

No matter what kind of an organization you are running, you better have a "Make Sure" list. Break through all the nonsense, and list the things that make the difference in your organization. There are a lot of ways to go on this one. I was a coach and an athletic director. I used to make a big deal out of my "Make Sure" list for coaches. If you cover all your bases, you should be set up for success. The following is a "Make Sure" list for any coach.

1. **Make Sure** you have a basic philosophy about how you want to coach your team.
2. **Make Sure** you have a big picture plan.
3. **Make Sure** your players are safe.
4. **Make Sure** you evaluate talent fairly and accurately.
5. **Make Sure** your players are in game condition.
6. **Make Sure** you have a sound game plan.
7. **Make Sure** your players know what to do.
8. **Make Sure** you are motivating your players.
9. **Make Sure** your players are focused.
10. **Make Sure** your players understand the expectations.
11. **Make Sure** your team executes.
12. **Make Sure** your players understand pressure.
13. **Make Sure** you prepare for unusual situations.
14. **Make Sure** your players hustle.
15. **Make Sure** your team shows sportsmanship and class.
16. **Make Sure** you have an evaluation process.

The Last 5 Minutes

"You have to expect things before you can do them."
--Michael Jordan

How many times have you seen a team totally control a game then lose it at the end? It happens all the time from the little leagues to the pros. Doesn't it make sense to address how to handle the end of the game, and make a plan for a strong finish?

Factor the end of the game into the plan. I wish that I would have addressed this issue more when I was coaching. I didn't. The first thing to do is to recognize the situation. Talk about it openly with your players. Have a plan to kill time off the clock if needed. Have your hurry up offense ready. Be sure everyone knows how to handle time outs. Try to think of everything that could happen and address it.

Be ready if the score isn't close. Address how your team will handle itself when you are on either side of a lopsided score. What will be happening on the sideline? How will your team conduct themselves? It doesn't matter whether you are winning or losing. You can avoid an embarrassing situation if you just address it with your players. If you make a plan and talk about it, it will work.

Act like you have been there before. You hear that quote all the time, but do you know the problem with that statement? The fact is that **most kids haven't been there before.** You are dealing with kids. Don't take anything for granted. There aren't that many kids out there that have scored a game winning touchdown in a varsity game. It's his first experience in that situation. Think about it! Counsel all the players on how to handle it.

It's your job as the coach to think of everything. The difference between ignorance and stupidity is simple. Ignorance means you have never been exposed to something. You don't know anything about it. Stupidity is when you have been exposed to something, and you still use poor judgment. If people have information and guidance, they usually do the right thing.

Be ready for close games. Emphasize to your team the importance of the last five minutes of **any** game. When the clock ticks down to the last five minutes, your team has a unified mindset. Address all situations. Take time to reinforce the importance of finishing the game off with strength. The players will realize a sense of urgency when the last five minutes are emphasized by the coaching staff.

A strong leader tries to think of everything. Your plan for the last five minutes might only make a difference one time all year. However, that may be the game that defines you.

Exude Confidence All the Way through Game Day

"Some pursue happiness, others create it." Unknown

Everybody is watching the head coach on game day. How he handles himself is critical to success. The most important time for the head coach is when he addresses the team before, during and after the game. A good head coach knows this. He plans everything out as well as he can. It makes a huge difference if he is prepared properly. It also gives him a chance to separate himself from the head coach on the other side.

Plan everything, and make sure everyone knows the plan. You can take a lot of pressure off the players and coaches if you plan everything. Take all the thinking away. Let everyone focus on his job. Emphasize to the coaches and players they should have no questions as to what is going to happen next. Everything is taken care of already. Everybody knows exactly when to meet, leave for the stadium, and go through pre-game warm-ups. Plan all the way to when the bus gets back to the gym and when the next meeting or practice is scheduled.

Make sure every rule is addressed. For example, I never believed in practice shoes and game shoes. In football, you wear the shoes that you wear, period. You might have multiple pairs, but you should never try to break in a brand new pair of cleats during a game. That's crazy. That goes for any uniform issue. If players don't wear gloves during practice, they shouldn't wear gloves in a game. The players have to get through all the uniform nonsense. Remember, it's a uniform not a costume.

You must show confidence. Every leader needs to be himself. He should use his personality as an asset. Some people are quiet.

Some people are emotional. However, whatever personality you have must have one important ingredient. ***You must show confidence.*** Tell the players something even if you aren't sure about it yourself. It isn't what you say but how you say it that will make the difference. They will probably forget your words, but they won't forget your confidence. If the head coach doesn't show confidence, how can the players show confidence?

A good coach has more influence right before kickoff than at any other time. Everyone on the team is focused and ready. It's a very emotional time. Memories that last a lifetime are often made right before going out for the kickoff. Make the statements that last at this time. Use your influence to cement positive, lasting thoughts in your player's minds.

Think ahead about Half-Time. Prepare for half-time all week. What is the weather going to be like? What can we do to be ready when the kids walk in the door? What is our system for using the press box? Who is breaking down routes? What is our communication system? How are we going to evaluate statistics? Give everyone on the staff a specific role at half-time. Keep everybody busy.

Let the players rest. Don't jump right into strategy sessions with the kids. Tell them beforehand that there might not be any half-time adjustments. Many times half-time adjustments aren't even necessary. The game isn't all that complicated.

In Texas, half-time might last 45 minutes because of the band and the drill team performances. The teams actually play doubleheaders. They play the first game. They take an extended break, and then they come back and play the second game. It is smart to develop a mindset like that. It is even possible the game could go into overtime. Then you would play a tripleheader.

Be organized for breaks. Make sure you have a set plan for the coaches to meet and then talk to the players. Explain to the coaches exactly what you want from them. Don't try to reinvent the wheel at half-time. It will only confuse the players. Use whatever system you choose. Just get some type of a plan on how you will use it effectively. Make sure the assistant coaches are a reflection of the head coach. They should be confident and prepared not shaky and unorganized.

Have multiple speeches ready. If you are a good leader, you will never take anything for granted. When you come in at half-time or after a game, you could be in any situation. Make sure you have thought out or better yet, written out, what you will say to the kids. Never be in a situation where you are at a loss for words. Have a check list that addresses these situations.

Half-time
1. way ahead
2. way behind
3. tied
4. close game either way
5. unexpected injuries
6. bad calls
7. more physical than we thought
8. gave up a score at the end of the half
9. fights or trash talking
10. crazy crowd

Post-game
1. easy win
2. blowout loss
3. disappointing loss
4. upset win
5. bad call
6. missed field goal
7. turnover that cost the game
8. blunder by the coaches

9. loss on the last play
10. win on the last play

Plan how to handle the media. Be totally prepared to address the media. Be prepared for the situations as above. It's your duty to talk to the media, but you can control what you say and how you say it. Never give excuses. Never make negative comments about referees. Never say anything negative about either your team or the opponent. Assign a coach you really trust to confront you before you go in to meet with the media. Make sure you have calmed down.

Get everyone home safely. If someone rides to the game on the bus, he should ride back to school on the bus. Sometimes there are exceptions, but there shouldn't be many. It is team building time, no matter what happens. Everyone should decompress together. We used to bring the kids in on Saturday morning. We would watch the film and learn from our mistakes. That was the main reason we met. However, I never discounted the fact that if we lost a tough game I didn't want to wait all weekend to communicate with the team. It was critical for morale to stay together. If you are the head coach, you better think about how you are going to react and conduct yourself. Don't ever forget, players reflect their head coach. We used to have a saying, "The game isn't over until we watch the film on Saturday morning." After the film, put the game to bed. Give the kids closure and move on.

Until Next Time

Until Next Time

"I like the dreams of the future better than the history of the past."
--Thomas Jefferson

I hope you have enjoyed this book. It took me years to complete it. In the end, it didn't turn out anything like I expected. I changed formats several times. I must have re-written it ten times. My family thought I would never follow through and publish it. One night at the dinner table my youngest son, Collin, challenged me, "Dad," he said, "you are all hat and no cattle. When are you actually going to finish this book?" He knew exactly what he was doing. I owe him, because that was the moment I decided to give myself a deadline and finish. Telling people you are writing a book is awkward, but going to print is downright scary. In the end, though, it was a lot of fun. Here is what I learned.

You have to have a purpose. I'm an old high school English teacher. I love to read and write. It was natural for me to want to express myself in book form. I never have thought I knew all the answers. I don't know if anyone will agree with anything I say. I just took the time to write it down.

My purpose was to get this book into the high school classroom. You might notice there is no profanity and nobody gets thrown under the bus. I tried hard to have perfect syntax, but every time I read through the book, I found a mistake somewhere. I also thought I might be able to write about some things that would entertain and maybe help people of all ages. This book has a lot of stuff about coaching, but coaching is just like any other business. It is about people.

179

Be a planner. One of the best quotes I have ever heard came from Abraham Lincoln. He said, "If I had eight hours to cut down a tree, I would spend the first six sharpening my axe." Most people don't like to plan. However, planning is what separates the pretenders from the contenders. At first, I jumped in and just started writing. I just had to go back and start over again. I ended up writing it just like my old English teachers taught me.

Understand how to evaluate. Writing is just talking on paper. That is all it is. You also must understand the best way to judge a book. If someone picks it up and reads all the way through, it's probably pretty good.

A book is just a bunch of pages bound together. A good book is one that is read cover to cover. When the reader longs for more after finishing, that's a great book.

Trust your instincts. There are points about faith scattered throughout this book. If I believe anything, I believe that we all should pray and trust our instincts. That is one way that God can talk to us.

The 70-30 Split. The makeup of a team is 70% the players and 30% the coaching. This book focused mainly on the coaching part. Strong leadership is the wild card that gives a team an advantage over the competition. The key is to know how to lead. Strong leaders ask the hard questions and stomach the tough answers. They are the number one trainer for their organization. They make sure everyone knows their agenda and how they plan on implementing it. As the competition level rises, the 70-30 split tightens. In the biggest games the coaching of the team is almost as important as the personnel. However, strong leaders know that they will never be more important than the players.